letters to america

a chance for us to listen

letters to america

a chance for us to listen

**Edited by Erica Geller
in Collaboration with Maggie Holmes**

Photography by Mark Brecke

RIVERWOOD BOOKS
Ashland, Oregon

Cover design by Mike Davis
Cover by David Ruppe, Impact Publications
Interior design by Gary Kliewer
Cover photo by Mark Brecke

Printed in Korea

Library of Congress Cataloging-in-Publication Data
Letters to America : a chance for us to listen / edited by Erica Chawn
Geller, in collaboration with Maggie Holmes ; photography by Mark
Brecke.
p. cm.
ISBN 1-883991-95-1 (pbk.)
1. United States--Foreign public opinion. 2. United
States--Civilization. 3. National characteristics, American. I.
Geller, Erica Chawn. II. Holmes, Maggie.
E169.12.L456 2004
303.48'2'090511--dc22
2003025079

A NOTE FROM THE EDITOR

The title *Letters to America* makes an incredible assumption. Obviously, the United States is not the only American country. There are at least 39 other countries that are also American nations. The words "America" and "American" that are being used to refer to the United States and its citizens have become an "idea." To many people, the idea of America is quite different than the reality of the United States. It is the idea of "America" that the authors of this book are addressing. While researching this topic online, I was introduced to a simple notion—the hope that we United States citizens will pursue the clarification of our country's self-description and establish ourselves as part of a community of American nations.

M. Brecke

TABLE OF CONTENTS

INTRODUCTION

Dear Friends,

For almost two years, I collected letters addressed to the American people and was introduced to hundreds of perspectives from all over the world. These impressions have significantly changed the way I perceive the United States' role on the planet and brought me a profound sense of the equality inherent in all human beings. I am honored to bring them to you in this collection.

The authors of these letters to America were found through the Internet, nongovernmental organizations, and friends, as well as by word of mouth. I asked contributors to speak from their hearts and to invite us into their shoes. They were each asked, "How is the United States impacting your life? If you could say anything to us, what would you say? What do you think we can do differently? What can we learn from each other?" I asked them to explore their opinions and to discover the reasons behind their feelings. This inquiry cultivated responses about America the idea, America the people, America the government, and America the culture.

This collection only represents one author per featured country, but the letters were not chosen to represent the consensus opinion of an entire nation. They were chosen based on the author's ability to bring us into his

Letters to America is for all of us who are ready to transform our "them" way of thinking into a "we" way of being.

or her unique experience. Each letter is a chance for us to learn about the far reaching effects of U.S. citizens' actions and decisions and is a chance for us to consider our important role in the global community. Although addressed to the people of America, this book is not just for Americans to hear the voices of our fellow humans around the world. *Letters to America* is for all of us who are ready to transform our "them" way of thinking into a "we" way of being.

In summer 2001, my dear friend Maggie Holmes and I came up with the idea for *Letters to America*. We created a Website to help facilitate the collection of letters and to spread the word about our call for submissions. Since then, over 600 people have submitted responses to *Letters to America*. I have had the opportunity to learn about international perspectives from the personal experiences in these letters. Before this project, I gave little attention to the world outside of my small personal sphere. But one day, it was as if I had opened my eyes for the first time. It was time then to learn about what was happening outside of myself, outside of my door, and outside of my country.

I grew up in a small, affluent town in Connecticut that was filled with community spirit and smiling white faces. There was a sense among us that we should help those less fortunate than ourselves. I carried a UNICEF collection box around on Halloween nights alongside my enormous sack of candy. But looking back, I realize that I did not know what UNICEF actually did. I wasn't shown a true reason to care. Thinking globally was not the way I was shown to focus my awareness. Instead, I was taught to strive for independent success.

It was not until I was 21 years old and I ventured to the Middle East that I realized the significant level of isolation experienced by U.S. citizens, compared to other citizens of the world. When I was in southern Turkey, I met a beautiful 11-year-old girl from Kyrgyzstan who knew much more about U.S. foreign policy than I did. I remember walking with her along a drying creek bed, sheepishly pretending to know where her homeland was on the map. Her exposure to American politics was shocking. She told me that people had harsh opinions about the U.S. and suggested that I would have an easier time

When I was in southern Turkey, I met a beautiful 11-year-old girl from Kyrgyzstan who knew much more about U.S. foreign policy than I did.

making my way from Istanbul to Cairo if I pretended to be Canadian. I chuckled and agreed, but on the inside, I was sad and confused. Why is it like this? Why didn't I know it is like this? As I continued to encounter new faces and accents, I noticed that almost everyone had an opinion about the U.S. I felt animosity from the Canadians toward America. They made good-humored jokes about the American tourists and wore Canadian flags on their packs to make sure they were not mistaken for U.S. citizens. I remember thinking, "Why would Canadians not like Americans? We don't even think about them." Of course! How appalling that we don't even think about them!

When I recognized this U.S. isolation and my global naiveté, I felt left out of the rest of the world. It was as if everyone had a big private joke about the United States. I did not feel a part of the global community. I understood for the first time that, for much of the world, I was one of "them." I felt a mixture of pride, shame, and confusion.

My hope for Letters to America is that it will provide an empathic experience along the path toward universal connectedness.

I recognize now that something was left out of my education: I was never taught about the value of universal empathy. Now that I'm looking out at the world, I see that equality, among every one of us, is essential for peaceful coexistence. Empathy creates equality. My hope for *Letters to America* is that it will provide an empathic experience along the path toward universal connectedness.

When we experience empathy, inequality cannot maintain

itself. An ingredient essential for successful empathy is the openness to recognizing that we all have the same core emotions and needs. I hope that you will read these letters with that same openness, and that, as a world, we can let the experiences of our fellow humans enter our hearts and minds so that we might realize our undeniable sameness.

Letters to America is a chance for us to listen.

We have the choice to live conscious of our true equality. This collection is forty-six opportunities to experience empathy, a chance to make that choice. The citizens of the world have shared their voices with the American people. *Letters to America* is a chance for us to listen.

In Peace,
Erica

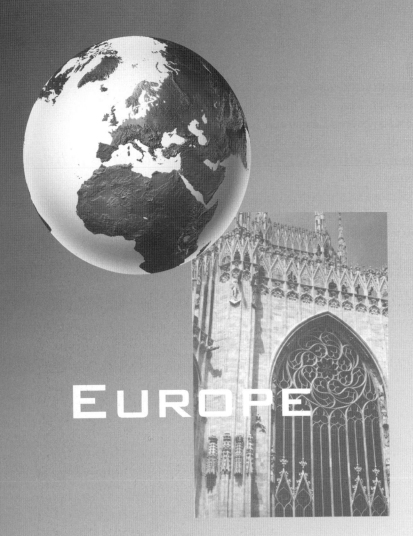

EUROPE

***0,67 EUR

ROMANIA

UKRAINE

BULGARIA

ENGLAND

PORTUGAL

ICELAND

BOSNIA AND
HERZEGOVINA

DENMARK

FRANCE

IRELAND

M. Brecke

BY AIR MAIL
PAR AVION

ROMANIA

WHERE	Southeastern Europe, bordering the Black Sea, between Bulgaria and Ukraine
SIZE	237,500 sq km, slightly smaller than Oregon
POPULATION	22,355,551 (July 2004 est.)
INFANT MORTALITY	27.24 deaths/1,000 live births
THE PEOPLE	Romanian 89.5%, Hungarian 6.6%, Roma 2.5%, Ukrainian 0.3%, German 0.3%, Russian 0.2%, Turkish 0.2%, other 0.4%
RELIGIONS	Eastern Orthodox (including all sub-denominations) 87%, Protestant 6.8%, Catholic 5.6%, other (mostly Muslim) 0.4%, unaffiliated 0.2%
LANGUAGES	Romanian, Hungarian, German
LITERACY RATE	Total population: 98.4% male: 99.1% female: 97.7% (2003 est.)
GOVERNMENT	Republic
CAPITAL	Bucharest

2

KINGA SIMO

ROMANIA

22 YEARS OLD, FEMALE, COLLEGE STUDENT

Dear People of America,

Being raised in a country where all options were, and still are in some ways, limited to the communist ideas, America is what we as kids imagined to be the promised land of the Bible. Now at my age, it is simply the land of possibilities. My great grandfather went to America in 1910 and returned after ten years. He was able to build a better life, to buy land for all his four daughters—a feat which would have been impossible otherwise. Those ten years he worked in an American cement factory caused blindness, yet he never regretted it. He was like a legend in our family. If he was able to give up on the light of his eyes just to be able to assure a better life for his children, what should I do for my future and for my future family?

The difference between the level of development in America and Romania is as great as it was 100 years ago. I totally gave up on the hope that it will ever really change. But one thing I know: I don't want my children to grow up as we did.

I am a Romanian citizen, but Hungarian by nationality. I wish I would have been born in a country like America where I believe people are more open minded about this kind of thing. I am aware that you American people had and may still have problems related to racial matters, but

M. Brecke

whenever I got the chance to talk to American people they always seem more open-minded than people around here. Growing up in a village with Romanian majority, I was once beaten by a Romanian older girl just because of my identity. She thought that my being Hungarian and she being Romanian gave her the right to be aggressive. I was afraid to tell my parents about this. I thought that it was their fault that they were Hungarians and that I did something wrong by speaking my own language. Some time was necessary for me to understand that it wasn't really my fault. And then it came to me. I wondered: why do I have to live here? Why couldn't I live in another country? And what country would you think that expresses more tolerance and freedom of speech and thinking than America? Let me tell you there is no other country with a greater image in a child's mind than America.

You should learn from our mistakes as human beings. You could try to be more tolerant than we are.

Here in Romania, there are some people who have a great fortune and an easy life like yours. Why do you think these people are ready to give up on so much to go to America? You may think that it is to gain an even greater fortune or an easier life. But it's not. It is the perception of what America means in our minds. America means having human rights. It means being innocent until proven guilty—a concept almost unknown here, at least until a few years ago. Even now that there have been ten years since the communists ruled our country, some concepts are still in peoples' minds, and maybe they will never be erased in this lifetime.

4

You are curious what you might learn from my country? You should learn from our mistakes as human beings. You could try to be more tolerant than we are. I am human so I make mistakes that I regret. Sometimes I am less civilized than I would like to be. These are the times when I wish I would be more like an American, for everything this concept means to me.

There is always something we can do to make a difference.

Your country also has some negative impacts on my life personally. As your economy is growing to be stronger, the inflation here keeps on making our lives harder and harder. It is just logical that the exchange rate for the U.S. dollar is growing while my parents income is becoming less and less. But I still have to pay my tuition in U.S. dollars. Whose life is getting harder by this? Mine, of course. This is one of the negative things about America. It concerns me that America has too large an impact on the lives of East European and other less developed countries.

My advice to you is: Don't you ever forget that we are all in the darkness sometimes. We stare from our eyes, we stumble, we hesitate, and we wonder, "Now what?" But there is a light at the end of the tunnel. We are each responsible for the light or darkness of our soul. There is always something we can do to make a difference.

Sincerely,

Kinga Simo

Ukraine

WHERE	Eastern Europe, bordering the Black Sea, between Poland and Russia
SIZE	603,700 sq km, slightly smaller than Texas
POPULATION	47,732,079 (July 2004 est.)
INFANT MORTALITY	20.61 deaths/1,000 live births
THE PEOPLE	Ukrainian 77.8%, Russian 17.3%, Belarusian 0.6%, Moldovan 0.5%, Crimean Tatar 0.5%, Bulgarian 0.4%, Hungarian 0.3%, Romanian 0.3%, Polish 0.3%, Jewish 0.2%, other 1.8%
RELIGIONS	Ukrainian Orthodox—Moscow Patriarchate, Ukrainian Orthodox—Kiev Patriarchate, Ukrainian Autocephalous Orthodox, Ukrainian Catholic (Uniate), Protestant, Jewish
LANGUAGES	Ukrainian, Russian, Romanian, Polish, Hungarian
LITERACY RATE	Total population: 99.7% male: 99.8% female: 99.6% (2003 est.)
GOVERNMENT	Republic
CAPITAL	Kiev (Kyyiv)

Mark Letichevsky

Ukraine

80 years old, male, retired editor

Dear People of America,

I was born in this city of Cherkassy, Ukraine, and spent almost all my eighty years of life here. Journalist by profession, I had been working in editorial offices of the local newspapers. I am a veteran of the Second World War.

I perceive America as a big and great country. During the years of war we were together fighting against our common enemy—fascism. Our common struggle and the meeting of the allies on Elba gave hope that our countries and peoples would keep together in and after war times. But the nuclear weapons race began (you began this race, dropping your first atom bombs on Hiroshima and Nagasaki). Then the cold war between our countries began.

I, personally, understand that the relationship of our countries was decided not by the ordinary people, but by politics. Ordinary people always wish to live in peace and prosperity.

Concerning the nowadays policy of the U.S.A.: sometimes it arouses not only my astonishment, but even indignation. You believe you should decide the fates of all nations, obtrude your will upon them, and intrude into the inner affairs of the sovereign countries. Acting in this way you by no means can find love and respect of the people in the world.

Here is an example. Your president didn't like the president of Yugoslavia—Miloshevich. He demanded Miloshevich to leave, and when he refused, the air force of NATO, where the U.S.A. plays the main role, literally destroyed this sovereign country. Not only were military targets bombed, but such civil objects like plants, houses, bridges, and hundreds and thousands of peaceful citizens. The Dunay river still cannot be navigated; countries near the Dunay carried extraordinary losses. And what was the result? By the help of your bombs and rockets, Albanian separatists came to power in Kosovo. They used America to tear off their part of Yugoslavia. Now they intrude even into the sovereign Macedonia. Such state of things is being condemned by many people in different countries, including Ukraine.

I can observe the culture of your country by watching your films that literally fill up the screens of our cinemas and TVs. In general, these are films about fighting, continuous shooting, murders, and violence. I understand that they are commercial films; they are being made for the sake of money. But they do not add to the authority of your culture. I can't understand why, for the sake of money, your culture is infiltrated by slapdash work which brings harm to society and to the upbringing of youth.

Your foreign policy and economic model contributed much to the disintegration of the Soviet Union. Now I am living

Acting in this way you by no means can find love and respect of the people in the world.

in an independent country, in Ukraine, which earlier was a republic of USSR. During our ten years of independence, life grew worse for the people here; it became miserable.

Until 1991, my family lived well in financial means. Since then, the material conditions of my family got considerably worse. My wife and I have received 324 grivnas pension for both of us ($60). This sum was hardly enough even for food; we have had to give up the most necessary things. We haven't bought clothes or shoes for ten years. My *We haven't bought clothes or shoes for ten years.* son and the elder grandson (he is twenty-three years old) have not been able to find a work for a long time. They are living on the money earned by the wife of my son. Many people (engineers, teachers, doctors, workers) have to resell things in the market. Our industry has gotten stuck, our economy doesn't work. No perspective of a good future can be seen.

But now a small group of people have found themselves able to do business (mostly by unfair means), and now they live a rich, luxurious life. They are surely feeling fine.

Of course, now there is nothing left for you to learn from my country. But, instead, many of the crooks here are learning from you how to do business. In America, capital has been accumulated with the help of unfair, sometimes even criminal ways. It starts being accumulated here this way as well. For example, with the help of dishonest state factories, power plants are being grasped for a trifling sum.

As for the spiritual and religious values of Americans—I am not of a high opinion about them. I understand that you have a lot of respectable people who guard their honest name and will never go against their conscience and do a mean thing. But most of the Americans find money a good substitution for God and it is to be obtained by any means. By the way, we are having many look-alike people appearing here now as well. I think they are learning this from you. They are ready to do anything for money. Still, many of them consider themselves a religious people, respectable Christians. This, of course, is incompatible with their disgraceful acts.

But most of the Americans find money a good substitution for God and it is to be obtained by any means.

America is a big, powerful, rich country. Many prominent scientists had left our country for yours in hope of a prosperous life. You were able to create a powerful economy that provides quite a high level of life for people. You were lucky that during war-times not a single bomb or missile was dropped on your territory. This has certainly helped the quick development of your economy. The Soviet Union, as with most of the European countries, had to lift their lands from ruins, which took much time and strength.

Here is the advice that I can give you. Although you are really rich and powerful … stop bragging of that and be more modest. Don't obtrude your will and your values onto others. Don't intrude into the affairs of other countries. If you want to help somebody, do it without humiliating them. Hold yourself with others like equals. Because when this disaster of September the 11th happened, the majority of people from earth sympathized with you, felt sorry for those who have died. In Moscow, people were carrying flowers to the American embassy. But some young people carried a poster, where it was written: "A reminder of Yugoslavia."

Everybody now understands that the U.S.A. is vulnerable too. Before September 11th we all considered America to be over the ocean and untouchable.

If you will be more modest and respect other big or little nations, then you will be doing a service to the world.

Sincerely,

Mark Letichevsky

BULGARIA

WHERE	Southeastern Europe, bordering the Black Sea, between Romania and Turkey
SIZE	110,910 sq km, slightly larger than Tennessee
POPULATION	7,517,973 (July 2004 est.)
INFANT MORTALITY	21.31 deaths/1,000 live births
THE PEOPLE	Bulgarian 83.6%, Turk 9.5%, Roma 4.6%, other 2.3% (including Macedonian, Armenian, Tatar, Circassian) (1998)
RELIGIONS	Bulgarian Orthodox 83.8%, Muslim 12.1%, Roman Catholic 1.7%, Jewish 0.1%, Protestant, Gregorian-Armenian, and other 2.3%
LANGUAGES	Bulgarian, secondary languages closely correspond to ethnic breakdown
LITERACY RATE	Total population: 98.6% male: 99.1% female: 98.2% (2003 est.)
GOVERNMENT	Parliamentary democracy
CAPITAL	Sofia

DENA POPOVA

BULGARIA

15 YEARS OLD, FEMALE, HIGH SCHOOL STUDENT

Dear People of America,

I am writing to you from my little country on the Balkan Peninsula, named Bulgaria. I was born fifteen years ago and so long I have lived only in Bulgaria. There are things that can be felt only by a Bulgarian in Bulgaria, very unique and precious for me.

Every morning when I leave home, I walk through one spacious meadow with many bushes and trees. It sounds like a fairy tale but it is true. When I get to the bus stop, I buy one cheese patty and eat it while I am waiting for the bus. When it comes, I get on it and I start watching the view that I watch every morning and that I know by heart. I know all the buildings, the trees, the parks that are on the way, but I never get bored. Every morning it is more interesting for me.

When I was younger, maybe five or six years old, I really admired your country. I had one Barbie doll and I knew it was made in America. I really loved it. Its name was Sindy. I behaved with her like she was alive. I cut her hair and waited for it to grow again. In fact it didn't grow and Sindy stayed with very short hair for the rest of her life. But she was still the most beautiful "girl" in the world because she was born in America. I had

also one very colorful shirt that was made in America. I didn't want to wear it because I wanted to keep it and to wear it when I go to America one day. I thought that everything that came from America was beautiful.

I didn't know where America was, how big it was, who lived there, what it was. America was just the whole world outside Bulgaria. Everything in America was beautiful and everyone there was happy. America was a dream. As I grew up, I understood more things about America. Now I know where it is, what it is, who lives there. Now America for me is something more normal, but it is still a place where most of the people are happy and there is not so much misery.

My great grandmother's dream is to visit America. Sometimes when I go to see her she asks me questions about America. She hasn't studied geography, and her favorite question is, "How far is America?" I always say, "It is nearer to the sun than Bulgaria," and she says, "Aha … because of that the Americans live so easy and well."

Every day when I turn on the TV, I hear something about America or about Americans. Almost all the things that I know about America are from the TV. America is part of our daily life, and most Bulgarians want to be like the Americans because they think that in this way they will succeed. I guess most of the people all round the world think this way. They think that in the American way of living every thing is easy and nice.

Try to make your country really the place where everyone can find happiness—the country that is more near to the sun than the others.

I don't know how it is in fact. But my advice to you, People of America … well, it is not exactly advice, but a wish: Try to make your country really the place where everyone can find happiness—the country that is more near to the sun than the others.

Sincerely yours,

Dena Popova

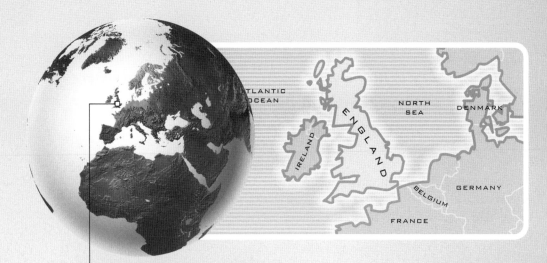

UNITED KINGDOM

WHERE	In Western Europe, islands including the northern one-sixth of the island of Ireland between the North Atlantic Ocean and the North Sea, northwest of France
SIZE	244,820 sq km, slightly smaller than Oregon
POPULATION	59,778,002
INFANT MORTALITY	5.45 deaths/1,000 live births
THE PEOPLE	English 81.5%, Scottish 9.6%, Irish 2.4%, Welsh 1.9%, Ulster 1.8%, West Indian, Indian, Pakistani, and other 2.8%
RELIGIONS	Anglican 29%, Roman Catholic 10%, other Christian churches 14%. Muslim 2.7%, Hindu 1%, Sikh 0.6%, Jewish 0.5%. Northern Ireland: Protestants 53%, Catholics 44% among Christian population.
LANGUAGES	English, Welsh (about 26% of the population of Wales), Scottish form of Gaelic (about 60,000 in Scotland)
LITERACY RATE	Total population: 99%
GOVERNMENT	Constitutional monarchy
CAPITAL	London

RUSSELL KENNEDY

ENGLAND – UNITED KINGDOM
30 YEARS OLD, MALE, CAMERA TECHNICIAN

Dear People of America,

I started writing this letter aboard a flight back to the U.K, from New York. It was my first visit to America and I flew on the day the allied coalition forces attacked Baghdad in Iraq on the second Persian Gulf War. It was a sobering thought when considering my opinions of America in the current political climate and our joint nations' impact on the Middle East. I wondered what I would discover on my short trip and how well my image of America fit the actuality. I grew up in England, and compared with most people in the world have had a privileged family upbringing with a good education.

I have never previously had the urge to visit the United States. There are too many other places of interest to see in the world, and having an image formed in my own mind of America, from the media or my own travelling experiences, I had been put off. Whether it was the extremely overweight and raucous sandal and baseball-cap-wearing tourists we all see in the major cities of the world, or the early-twenty-somethings backpacking around Europe. You are always the noisy ones who you can hear above everybody else, carrying a guitar on which you cannot play a note while trying to look oh so cool. Always self opinionated and always misinformed.

Always the ones people quietly laugh at! I had previously seen the stereotypes and did not want to know them.

You see, unfortunately the American people are seen as the laughing stock of the world. It may be the stereotype but it is an

opinion held throughout much of the western world and in the U.K. It is a widespread joke that the United States would be such a great place if it weren't filled with Americans!

Your nation is regarded as a paranoid, spoilt, trigger-happy, ill-informed and ill-educated child who is blinkered from the outside world. This child has everything, yet will snatch whatever it wants from whomever it wishes, whenever it cares to, or it will cry and bawl until it gets it. Stamping over anyone to reach its goal. Gullible and shallow. It thinks it is the greatest and safest country in the world. Invincible, right, just, and good.

In these presently fragile times I can see that my country will possibly be tarred with the same brush.

It is hard for me to comment on the impact of America on my country as it has been slowly influencing us for most of my life through fast food outlets or mass consumerism. But it is surely the media that has the biggest impact on my country and also the rest of the world. It is your biggest export and it fashions the world's view of America so strongly. Children play cops and robbers or cowboys and Indians with toy guns and imitate American accents. I used to do it. Living out the glamorous image that the TV has instilled in us. While this glossy ideal is

While this glossy ideal is so attractive to much of the world, it is very easy to see how many find it so offensive. The mass consumerism, greed, gluttony and sheer selfishness and over-use of resources...

so attractive to much of the world, it is very easy to see how many find it so offensive. The mass consumerism, greed, gluttony, and sheer selfishness and over-use of resources. I live in this sort of world and love it, but at the same time I cannot deny that this has helped me form my view of your country.

Recently I spent time in Thailand on a beautiful island where many young people came and went on their travels through southeast Asia. A place where life was simple and friendship came easily.

I was in a bar late one night where everyone would meet and party, and got chatting to an American guy who was about my age. I got on well with him and we talked for some time. He came across as a well-rounded and intelligent man, but then he said something that appalled me.

He started to explain to me how great his country was and how it should stay that way. In his opinion, America HAD to have oil. It would stop functioning without it, and it was America's GOD-GIVEN RIGHT to take the oil it needed from wherever it could, by whatever means. I was utterly shocked and our conversation ended there, I had no desire to speak to him anymore. I found it appalling that in this day and age a member of my generation, a generation that has been brought up to question things, and a man who seemed so intelligent, could have such backward and blinkered views. It was as if he was travelling the world and taking no notice of what he saw.

It saddened and shocked me and worried me that he is probably one of the majority that have such a narrow view yet have so much influence in the world and therefore so much power. He spoke with such a shallow naivety, yet was so convinced that he was right—and that is how Americans are sometimes viewed. He was scratching the surface with so little understanding. Rewriting the world rather than finding the harmonisation and integration that could exist. He believed his own press and did not understand the irony of what he was saying.

Maybe the atrocity of September 11 proved to the American people that they are not invincible. It proved that you were not immune to terrorist attack and ripped away the cotton wool that you've had wrapped around yourself for so long. Maybe this has awakened the people of your nation and mine to their foreign policies and images abroad and the consequences of these policies. If this is so, then a lot of good will come out of bad.

Have you, for example, wondered why bin-Laden attacked the U.S.A. on September 11th? Have you had the curiosity to study foreign policies of the last thirty years and to see what really happened in that part of the world or surrounding areas? Have you considered just why certain countries in the world are not too fond of the Western world? Do you know where these countries are on a map?

Do you even know of, or have you researched, what Pol Pot did in Cambodia in very recent history, or even *why* America got so deeply involved in Vietnam? Have you even questioned *who* helped to fund the IRA in their campaign of terrorism against the UK over the last thirty years or so? Have you looked at Moslem countries and their religion in order to try to

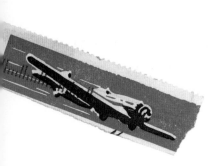

understand the culture and deep-seated history, or are they just the enemy because they are different?

It is hard for me to advise your nation as it is so similar to my own and I am not an authority in such matters, but if I could advise my advice would be to open up, look at a map and see the world. Realise that there is more than America on that map, discover it and see it first hand. Climb out the windowless box you live in and look around, see and enjoy the diversity and friendship that is out there.

America is full of really genuinely friendly and warm people. You have shown that to me on my recent visit and dispelled many myths. Just see that in other people. Your greatest strength is in your freedom to learn. Your greatest weakness is in not using this freedom. You have access to much of the world's knowledge through the Internet. My advice would

Your greatest strength is in your freedom to learn. Your greatest weakness is in not using this freedom.

be to use it to your advantage, use it as a tool of discovery and use it to broaden your horizons. Discover the world and its people, how wonderful they can be.

Respect it and enjoy it. Rid yourselves of the fear.

Sincerely,

Russell Kennedy

PORTUGAL

WHERE	Southwestern Europe, bordering the North Atlantic Ocean, west of Spain
SIZE	92,391 sq km, slightly smaller than Indiana
POPULATION	10,524,145 (July 2004 est.)
INFANT MORTALITY	5.13 deaths/1,000 live births
THE PEOPLE	Homogeneous Mediterranean stock; citizens of black African descent who immigrated to mainland during decolonization number less than 100,000; since 1990 East Europeans have entered Portugal
RELIGIONS	Roman Catholic 94%, Protestant 6%
LANGUAGES	Portuguese
LITERACY RATE	Total population: 93.3% male: 95.5% female: 91.3% (2003 est.)
GOVERNMENT	Parliamentary democracy
CAPITAL	Lisbon

SANDRA MARQUES

PORTUGAL

32 YEARS OLD, FEMALE, SCIENTIST

Dear People of America,

First of all, I would like to thank those of you I have met when I visited that were incredibly nice to me: the bus driver, the library attendant, the cleaning crew at the University. It is because of you, and because of what the U.S. used to stand for, and at times still does, that I fell in love with it. This is also why I have such great expectations and why I get so upset when I feel that, once again, decision making at the government level has nothing to do with the so-called "American values." Having come myself from a country that not so long ago was a dictatorship, I know how to distinguish between a people and the government. If the people have a good heart, there is hope. They put the government in place. But an ignorant people is a problem because they are easily manipulated.

The reasons for leaving the U.S.A. and finally returning home were many.

A big factor, though, was that I was becoming increasingly uncomfortable paying taxes to the Pentagon to help build bombs used to punish this and that person (once a friend, now a foe), such and such regime all over the world, causing "collateral damage" in the process. Collateral damage

Having come myself from a country that not so long ago was a dictatorship, I know how to distinguish between a people and the government. If the people have a good heart, there is hope.

happens to have names, kin, and unfortunately no more future. I felt guilty.

My American friends told me not to think about it. They said foreign policy was too complicated anyway and there was nothing anybody could do about it. But then I went home and watched PBS (I *love* PBS—don't let it die!) and learned about Lincoln and Jefferson and the bill of rights, and I began to feel American. I began to feel that loving America meant that I had to be involved and care. If there is one thing that is different in the States than in Portugal, it is the possibility of contact between rulers and people (other than during election time). This was also when I realized how tired the American people are. Over-worked and tired. I kept telling my friends back home that Americans are really good people. They are just naive. They don't like to think that their government does bad things in their name and they want to believe their president when they are told it has to be a certain way. They still believe in good versus evil, but as if the world were made of black and white and no gray. They are called upon to make decisions based on "digested" facts, which they have no idea how to verify. But if they find out about the true realities behind the "news" (it does happen from time to time), they do the right thing. They are like children and they care about suffering. They are just tired. It is no excuse, but it is different from saying they are "evil." They are *not* evil. I sensed some people thought of me as having become myself naïve, but they had not lived in the U.S. They did not go through the rollercoaster of loving it, hating it, loving it again, finally realizing you don't hate it—you are just disappointed. In a way, I get more disappointed at the U.S. than I get at my own country. I have higher expectations of the U.S.

I am going to marry an American, and I love his family. They are from Tennessee. I will make sure my kids celebrate the Fourth of July and know all there is to know about the U.S.A. I want them to be proud of where they come from and to share in the responsibility that comes with it. I will also make sure they are not afraid to speak their mind, to become unpopular because they profess an other-than-mainstream view.

> *In a way, I get more disappointed at the U.S. than I get at my own country. I have higher expectations of the U.S.*

I still have many hopes for the U.S. and the world. I will always love the good in it—and try to show the bad in it, because I care. Right now my country needs me more, so I will do my best here.

Sandra

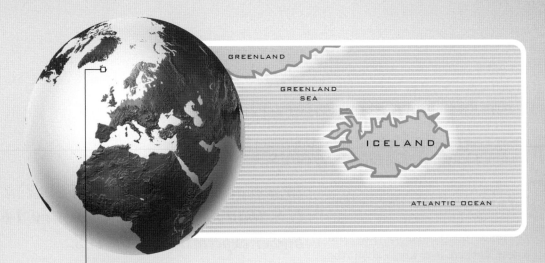

GREENLAND

GREENLAND
SEA

ICELAND

ATLANTIC OCEAN

ICELAND

WHERE	Northern Europe, island between the Greenland Sea and the North Atlantic Ocean, northwest of the U.K.
SIZE	103,000 sq km, slightly smaller than Kentucky
POPULATION	3,969,558 (July 2004 est.)
INFANT MORTALITY	5.5 deaths/1,000 live births
THE PEOPLE	Homogeneous mixture of descendants of Norse and Celts 94%, population of foreign origin 6%
RELIGIONS	Evangelical Lutheran 87.1%, other Protestant 4.1%, Roman Catholic 1.7%, other 7.1%
LANGUAGES	Icelandic, English, Nordic languages, German widely spoken
LITERACY RATE	Total population: 100% (2004 est.)
GOVERNMENT	Constitutional republic
CAPITAL	Reykjavik

Þórey Þórisdóttir

Iceland

19 years old, female, college student

Dear People of America,

I am writing to you from Iceland, an island situated between Norway and Greenland. I live in the heart of Iceland's capital, Reykjavik. I'm nineteen years old and my religion is the Old Norse religion, Ásatrú/Odinism. This was the true religion of Iceland before we were forced to take up Christianity about 1,000 years ago. I love living in Iceland. I can't really imagine living anywhere else.

There's a couple of things that make me wonder. For example, in Icelandic schools, kids are taught the basics about all the American states, people, land, and so on, while Americans aren't taught a thing about Iceland. I've often had an American ask me, "Is Iceland in Alaska?" or, "Iceland … you mean Norway?" It's disturbing, and at times insulting.

Now then, my opinion on America: I both love it and hate it, but it's like that with all countries. No country is perfect. I've read in books that people tend to get beat up or even killed if they like something that others don't approve of, and that rapists and murderers are freed more often than criminals who only stole something. I think that's just stupid and unfair. Perhaps it's like that in a lot of countries; I don't know. I've read a lot about

America because it's always on the news and such. But the one thing I dislike most is how so many Americans think so highly of themselves, claiming their country is the best in the world when they've not even been outside their own state. That really annoys me—probably because I really dislike close-minded people in general. But fortunately there are heaps of people who don't think like that, and I can only hope that even more people in America will be more open to other countries.

My parents have, of course, influenced my views a great deal, but I have my own opinions, too. My mother doesn't really know much about America; in fact, she's a bit scared of it. Why, though, I'm not sure. Maybe it's the size and the crime rate there. In Iceland, the crime rates are extremely low. A murder is a very rare thing, for example. My father has different views. Though he's never been to America, his views are mostly positive. He used to be a pilot and met many Americans back then. Sometimes he enjoys joking about how much of a hamburger-nation America is, what with all the news about America being the most overweight country in the world and such. I personally don't agree with his opinion. Sure, America is a "fat" country, but so are so many other countries. Iceland has overweight problems, too. In fact, if I remember hearing right, all of Scandinavia

But the one thing I dislike most is how so many Americans think so highly of themselves, claiming their country is the best in the world when they've not even been outside their own state.

has this exact same problem. But that doesn't change the people … though I've read that overweight people tend to be much happier than really skinny people. I think I'll agree on that; my experiences with bigger people have always been positive.

But yeah, it really disturbs me how so many Americans think they're better than other people. They think that America is the best country in the world, and that America is superior in every way. I can't help but feel that's irrational. Like I said before, no country is perfect, and no country will ever be perfect. I wish Americans would just accept that you're a great nation, and there's much you can do, but you're not perfect.

And here's an interesting fact! Iceland and America are alike in many ways. Both countries have loads of unspoiled nature, anything from deserts to forests. America, to me, is an amazing country really. It's so large and geographically diverse. I'm betting I could see a little bit of every country in the world if I traveled across America.

Anyhow, I hope I can one day visit America, both to travel there and to meet all the wonderful people I've met online through the years.

Best wishes from Þórey in Iceland

Bosnia and Herzegovina

WHERE	Southeastern Europe, bordering the Adriatic Sea and Croatia
SIZE	51,129 sq km slightly smaller than West Virginia
POPULATION	4,007,608 (July 2004 est.)
INFANT MORTALITY	21.88 deaths/1,000 live births
THE PEOPLE	Serb 37.1%, Bosniak 48%, Croat 14.3%, other 0.5% *Note*: Bosniak has replaced Muslim as an ethnic term in part to avoid confusion with the religious term Muslim—an adherent of Islam
RELIGIONS	Muslim 40%, Orthodox 31%, Roman Catholic 15%, Protestant 4%, other 10%
LANGUAGES	Croatian, Serbian, Bosnian
LITERACY RATE	Total population: 86.05% male 94.1% female 78.0%.
GOVERNMENT	Emerging federal democratic republic
CAPITAL	Sarajevo

ALMIR ZUKAN

BOSNIA AND HERZEGOVINA
30 YEARS OLD, MALE, UNEMPLOYED

Dear People of America,

I will use this opportunity to share my personal experience about your country.

First of all, I want to express my sadness about innocent victims of recent terrorist attacks at your country.

I'm born and live in country where a person can't be master of his own life. This is very sad. As we had war in past time, most of my family has gone to the United States as refugees. I have many letters between us and also with my American friends who are helping us during the war and after. Through them I see pictures of your lifestyle, which I deeply respect. Many of my relatives and friends on the day of leaving from Bosnia told me that they will return sometime in the future, but they changed their opinion now as they have lived a couple of years in the States. They are more self confident now and look at life from a different and better viewpoint. They don't think just about food as they did here. They can plan now their lives in advance, which is not the case here—where often people work today just to eat tomorrow. The main thing that I respect is that knowledge comes in first place when employment is in question, not like here, where many

Even small groups of people from your country can have a big impact in countries like mine, commenting on the situation here and what can be done to improve lives for people.

other reasons are in front of knowledge. My family said that in America they experienced, for the first time, that their name and religion didn't matter. It's not like here, where you can be killed just because you belong to another nationality or have a different opinion.

My best friend in your country is one American woman from Madera, California, named Jane. She has made great efforts to help my people. She is a bright light in our sad lives, showing that in spite of distance and lifestyle somebody exists who wants to make this world better by helping and advising people who need it desperately. And she expects nothing in return. I can't express by words all of what she does for my people and me. She saves peoples' lives here in many ways. Personally, she gave me needed strength to survive. God bless her. Before her, for me it was unthinkable that a person like that existed in the world.

Also, my sister lives in Virginia with her husband and two daughters. They are different nationalities, so they had a lot of problems here as people became separate as a result of the recent war. They found their happiness in your country. They told me nice things about your country—about equal rights, and that you are the owners of your life, which is not often the case in my country. I deeply respect American lifestyle.

I think that America can help in many ways, not just on a material bases. Even small groups of people from your country can have a big impact in countries like mine, commenting on the situation here and what can be done to improve lives for people. Our main hobby here is to survive in these hard times; even nice words mean a lot to us. Your biggest strength is "United" States. You work hard and earn enough for a decent life. Here, often people's quality doesn't mean anything because a lot of other things have influence, which is not case in your country.

I'm thirty and have never been abroad. Many of my people are standing in front of the embassies day and night to go somewhere on business, as a tourist, or for a student visa. It is hard to get out, and I hope it will be changed. I have a dream that I will visit my cousins and friends there someday. I hope that my dream will become truth. I'm very glad to hear that my friends and people from my country get a fair chance to succeed in your country. Here they didn't have a chance at all. Many of them are still supporting their families back here.

Here, our politicians absurdly talk about the prosperity of our country and how they believe in the future of this country, but all of them sent their children abroad where they study and work.

Anyway, hope still exists and never disappears.

Best wishes for American people from this part of the world,

Almir

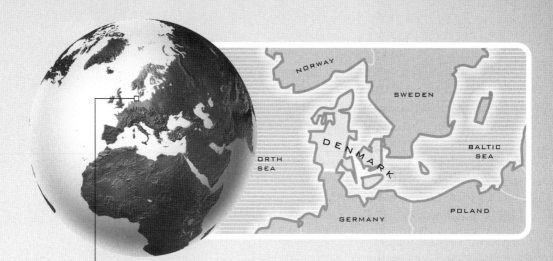

DENMARK

WHERE	Northern Europe, bordering the Baltic Sea and the North Sea, on a peninsula north of Germany (Jutland); also includes two major islands (Sjaelland and Fyn)
SIZE	43,094 sq km, slightly less than twice the size of Massachusetts
POPULATION	5,413,392 (July 2004 est.)
INFANT MORTALITY	4.63 deaths/1,000 live births
THE PEOPLE	Malay Scandinavian, Inuit, Faroese, German, Turkish, Iranian, Somali
RELIGIONS	Evangelical Lutheran 95%, other Protestant and Roman Catholic 3%, Muslim 2%
LANGUAGES	Danish, Faroese, Greenlandic (an Inuit dialect), German (small minority), *Note:* English is the predominant second language
LITERACY RATE	Total population: 100%
GOVERNMENT	Constitutional monarchy
CAPITAL	Copenhagen

SIMONA NIELSEN

DENMARK

33 YEARS OLD, FEMALE, E-ZINE AUTHOR STUDYING
WEB DESIGN

Dear People of America,

I have never been to the U.S.A., but I've had many American friends over the years. In our letters to each other we have laughed, cried, and fought, and I don't think they saw me any different from them. The differences are there, but we've always managed to stay friends.

A friend of mine went to the U.S.A. to work for a short while. It was his first time there. When he arrived, he called me to say that the trip went well. I asked him how America was so far, and he replied, "I have never seen so many fat people in my entire life!" That was the first thing he noticed. Okay, I have seen the Ricki Lake Show, so I believed him. America is the land of fast food. It seems to me that no one cares about their looks and health unless we talk about Hollywood. In Denmark we still cook our own food in our own kitchens. The kitchen is the rallying point of the family. When we go to work, we have a homemade, healthy lunch pack and fruits with us. We don't walk around a corner to buy a hot dog or a burger on our lunch break. In the U.S.A. there is fast food on every corner; you don't see that in Denmark. We have McDonald's—oh yeah—and our kids love it. I'm a parent and I try to be strong. I do take my kids to McDonald's once in a while, though.

You seem to be hysterically religious. You just have to believe in something. There are so many different beliefs and sects that I get really confused. If you want to explain to people why you succeeded or why you failed, you always end the speech by saying that God had something to do with it. In my country, we either believe or not. The Danes rarely mention God, not even when we go to church. Not many of us go to church on a regular Sunday, but that doesn't mean that we don't believe. As for myself, I carry my belief within my heart–like many Danes do.

I can go out without locking my door. I can place my bicycle and my dog (if I had one) outside a grocery store and both will still be there when I come out.

You think you have invented everything. One of my best American friends and I were chatting on the Internet and somehow we came to talk about Lego. She told me she used to play with Lego a lot when she was a kid. I told her Lego was Danish and hell broke loose! She and her husband laughed at me and said that Lego had to be American, and I had to tell them to go to Lego's home page before they believed me. In fact, you invented less than you think, so please give credit to the rest of the world.

I can go out without locking my door. I can place my bicycle and my dog (if I had one) outside a grocery store and both will still be there when I come out. When my kids were infants, I could place the baby carriage outside in my garden or outside a restaurant where I could see it from a window. That reminds me of a story that took place in New York a few years ago. A Danish mother visited her child's American father so he could spend some time with the kid. They went to a restaurant and placed the baby carriage right outside the restaurant window where they were sitting, so the child would be protected from the smoke in the restaurant. The New Yorkers were in shock when they passed this sight and called the police from their cell phones. The mother was arrested and put to trial for six months. The child was placed in family care. After the six months she could go back to Denmark with her baby, but with a huge warning on her back. I was shocked! Shocked about your fear, about the crime, about the environment you have to live in. Please do understand that it's normal to do things like that here, that we feel safe, that we can protect our children, that we don't feel the same fear.

Almost everyone can buy a gun in America. I don't understand that, but I do understand that it will cause much crime. I'm not saying that there is no crime here, but it's nothing compared to your country. America is also called Land of the Free—I wonder if that is true.

America is also called Land of the Free— I wonder if that is true.

Teens are getting pregnant all the time in America. Teens are proud members of gangs. It seems to me that it's a huge problem and that there is something missing in the families. Something to hold your families together. You use the phrase "I love you" a lot, but do you love hard enough? Do you pay enough attention to your children?

When I go to the doctor or the hospital, I don't have to bring money. I can get an operation without worrying how to pay for it. Everyone in this country must have a place to live and be able to keep up a decent standard of living. Welfare! Don't even mention it to the American people! If you receive welfare you are considered a low person. A loser! Well, not here. I pay half my income in taxes, so I believe I'm entitled to welfare when I need it. Everyone does. We have a very small group of homeless people, but they have chosen that themselves. They are allowed to receive welfare like anyone else. I don't have to save my money for my children's education; I pay that over taxes, too. In your country there are either rich or poor people. In mine, most of us belong to the middle class.

In your country there are either rich or poor people. In mine, most of us belong to the middle class.

I can really laugh when I hear that an American woman can sue a company for not saying in the instruction manual for her newly bought microwave oven that she shouldn't put her dog in there for a dry clean; and I can't believe she won, either! You can sue anyone for just being alive and even win. It is also said that America is the Land of Opportunities—and that could be right.

You would probably laugh when you hear us calling an area with 1 million inhabitants a city. In your eyes, it would probably be a town. Everything is bigger over there—huge.

Credit cards and shopaholics. There might be a few here, but still nothing compared to you. I guess you have learned to think "BIG," while I have learned to think "small." This makes me think of how easy it is for you to create huge companies with success. That is admirable. It's not easy to become rich in Denmark, but it seems easy for you.

You don't have a long history. Your country was built by immigrants–your ancestors. Knowing that fact, it amazes me that some of you think that Europe is one country, or that some of you don't know where my country is located–or that it's really a country. Some of you haven't even heard of Denmark.

I live in a monarchy. We have a Queen and her royal family to represent it. We have a Prime

Think before you start any wars and think before you judge other people.

Minister to rule it. I live in a democracy. We don't intervene in the world's big affairs much. We are a stubborn people, though, and always ready to support the best party. The U.S.A., for example.

I will encourage you to learn about other cultures. That people in other parts of the world live totally different lives from you. It seems like you only see your own "big" world and forget that you are not the only ones on the planet. Think before you start any wars and think before you judge other people.

Warm regards,

Simona Nielsen

FRANCE

WHERE	Western Europe, bordering the Bay of Biscay and English Channel, between Belgium and Spain, southeast of the U.K.; bordering the Mediterranean Sea, between Italy and Spain
SIZE	547,030 sq km, slightly less than twice the size of Colorado
POPULATION	60,424,213 (July 2004 est.)
INFANT MORTALITY	4.31 deaths/1,000 live births
THE PEOPLE	Celtic and Latin with Teutonic, Slavic, North African, Indochinese, Basque minorities
RELIGIONS	Roman Catholic 83%-88%, Protestant 2%, Jewish 1%, Muslim 5%-10%, unaffiliated 4%
LANGUAGES	French 100%, rapidly declining regional dialects and languages (Provencal, Breton, Alsatian, Corsican, Catalan, Basque, Flemish)
LITERACY RATE	Total population: 99% male: 99% female: 99%
GOVERNMENT	Republic
CAPITAL	Paris

NATHALIE COHEN

FRANCE

27 YEARS OLD, FEMALE, RETAIL MARKETER FOR NESTLÉ

Dear People of America,

I'm French and I love America; it can sound strange if we considered the current situation, but I do love you and your country. Yes, I'm against Bush's government, but Bush is not America and America is not Bush, so I've overlooked this war because I surely know that a war isn't a reflection of everyone's thoughts and wants. Moreover, I really think that it's a mistake to consider a country and its people as the reflection of its government. What should all the Israeli people say? Today, Israel has a bad international image (thanks to the media, by the way), but does all the Israeli population want this situation? Are they really agreeing with Ariel Sharon's policy? We don't know, but we cannot say that Israeli people are violent or whatever; we really need to overlook that. It's exactly the same with America.

All around me, there are people who are harshly criticizing you and your country. Why? Because of your image, the one that is used and used by the media: the richest and strongest nation in the world always attacks the poorest and weakest. On September 11, 2001, those people were quite happy because the power of America has been touched. Some people, who were actually my friends, said horrible things like, "They deserve it," or "It's

I'll always remember this homeless man in New York who kindly answered my brother, when he tried to give him a sandwich, "No thanks, I've already eaten, I just need a dessert."

their fault," and "They're not untouchable." It hurts me; it was horrible, but it's what I really heard. I know that it's the freedom of expression, but how? I decide to keep quiet; it was impossible to discuss with them. It changes something in how I consider them.

So why am I so attached to a country which is so criticized by those around me? As for me, I think that I really agree with your way of life. I also agree with some of your ideas, but not because of what my family thinks. I have my own thoughts and feelings. Moreover, I think that I am more attached to America than my parents are. But still, to be really honest, I'm sure that the fact that my family is Israeli influenced my opinion concerning your country; especially when we know that Israel is called "Little America." But I insist: *influenced, not obliged.*

I discovered America when I was thirteen years old, my first big trip, full of memories. What surprised me much were you, the American people, and your way of life. You're welcoming, nice, generous, and respectful. I'll always remember this homeless man in New York who kindly answered my brother, when he tried to give him a sandwich, "No thanks, I've already eaten, I just need a dessert." The way he said that was so natural but also so kind. It was so pleasant. You're true people, but I know you're not perfect—nobody is. You're arrogant and proud of yourself, maybe too much. "Showoffs" is a term that qualifies you well. It's true that when you do stuff everyone knows about it. Even during the war in Iraq, you had a need to tell what you're paying for and how many. And thanks to the media the entire world knows about you, maybe too much. Well, that is all the negative I can say about you, and you know what? Don't change it, because I really think that it's what makes you special and unique. Doesn't every country have the right to be unique?

We all need to learn things from each other because no one is living the same way.

I would be very happy if a part of the French people who criticized you change their mind or think differently. As for me, it will be fair to hear people say, "We aren't against America, we are against all countries which declares its hegemony," instead of, "I don't like America because Bush decided to attack Iraq." We'll see.

We all need to learn things from each other because no one is living the same way. I do have a different life from my neighbors, but each experience is filled with personal enrichment and moral lessons. If we decide to communicate with each other, there is so much to be gained. As for me, the French really need to learn from you your way of life, your sense of generosity and help, your friendliness, but also your sense of humor. You, the Americans, just need to learn one thing from us: how to make good bread!

Nathalie Cohen

IRELAND

WHERE	Western Europe, occupying five-sixths of the island of Ireland in the North Atlantic Ocean, west of Great Britain
SIZE	70,280 sq km, slightly larger than West Virginia
POPULATION	3,969,558 (July 2004 est.)
INFANT MORTALITY	5.5 deaths/1,000 live births
THE PEOPLE	Celtic, English
RELIGIONS	Roman Catholic 91.6%, Church of Ireland 2.5%, other 5.9%
LANGUAGES	English is the language generally used, Irish (Gaelic) spoken mainly in areas located along the western seaboard
LITERACY RATE	Total population: 98-99%
GOVERNMENT	Republic
CAPITAL	Dublin

44

Ruairi MacThiarnain

Ireland

24 years old, male, youth health researcher

Dear People of America,

When I finished my studies in management, I set off for a summer of fun and relaxation in San Francisco. When I got there, I wasn't let down, but was shocked to say the least. For the previous twenty-two years I had watched American movies, listened to your great music from blues to rock, read books from American authors such as Steinbeck, and listened eagerly to my professors who told me of your great and free society of equality and freedom. I soon discovered that these were very much half truths of a much bigger picture.

San Francisco is a rich city on all accounts. It's rich in monetary wealth, history, culture, and in diversity. In this small city, I was disgusted to find up to 15,000 homeless people lost in a forgotten warp of poverty, illness, and insanity. I found out that many of these people had fought as teenagers for your country in Vietnam and was shocked by the lack of personal, governmental, and societal compassion. I met with a brave few who tried to help them by giving them food and heard how these caring people were criminalized by a legal system that deemed them "trading without a permit." I saw how two giant corporate newspapers

It seemed to me to be a vast contrast of rich and poor, the powerful and the powerless, pop culture and real culture, and of lies and truths.

(I worked for one, initially) reported selected views, half-piece stories, and limited truths of people, places, and wars that I knew to be much different. I watched as students, young married couples, artists, and trades people were being pushed out of the city to make way for the dot-coms, the money, the power. It seemed to me to be a vast contrast of rich and poor, the powerful and the powerless, pop culture and real culture, and of lies and truths. I got depressed when I thought of the vast wealth that was being created and that wasn't being shared, but I gained hope when I learned of the fight for justice by a few courageous souls. That's San Fransico to me—an example of the worst element of your country (the money, the poverty, the greed, the power, the lies) and the most beautiful element (the music, the culture, the free street newspapers, the buzz, the history of struggle, the ethnic mix). Sadly, the beautiful element of the U.S. seems to be drowning in a sea of pressure, corruption, and lies. The bad guys are winning! What's more, your business-controlled government, media, and military seem intent on exporting this sickening cancer from your beautiful land. Don't be surprised if many of us around the world reject it or fight it. Many people here in Ireland and in Europe are saddened when we see what the U.S. is becoming and how it is acting, but I keep telling them to have faith. When they ask me why, I tell them, "It's only one side of a great country, and I, too, during my summer of love, witnessed the magic that's still there." Don't let them destroy the magic!

Sadly, the beautiful element of the U.S. seems to be drowning in a sea of pressure, corruption, and lies. The bad guys are winning!

All my love and support in your fight for true freedom,

Ruairi

MIDDLE EAST

تهران كوى نصر خيابان سى و سوم
طبق اول قنترل امنى
١٨
ایران
POST 5500 پلاک
مسعيد امنى مطلق
کد پستى ١٤٤٧٩

IRAQ

JORDAN

ISRAEL

IRAN

AFGHANISTAN

LEBANON

M. Brecke

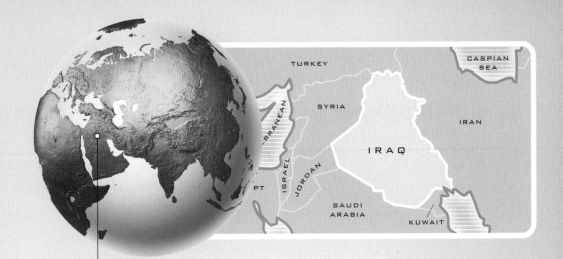

IRAQ

WHERE	Middle East, bordering the Persian Gulf, between Iran and Kuwait
SIZE	437,072 sq km, slightly more than twice the size of Idaho
POPULATION	25,374,691 (July 2004 est.)
INFANT MORTALITY	52.71 deaths/1,000 live births (July 2004 est.)
THE PEOPLE	Arab 75%-80%, Kurdish 15%-20%, Turkoman, Assyrian or other 5%
RELIGIONS	Muslim 97% (Shi'a 60%-65%, Sunni 32%-37%), Christian or other 3%
LANGUAGES	Arabic, Kurdish (official in Kurdish regions), Assyrian, Armenian
LITERACY RATE	Total population: 40.4% male: 55.9% female: 24.4% (2003 est.)
GOVERNMENT	In transition following April 2003 fall of Saddam Hussein regime by U.S.-led coalition
CAPITAL	Baghdad

Ghazwan Al-Mukhtar

Iraq
63 years old, male, Retired engineer

Dear People of America,

I do understand your sorrow for what happened Sep. 11. I, too, feel very sorry for losing lives of innocent people—whether in New York, Baghdad, or Bethlehem. And I know the aftermath of the death of innocent people is long lasting.

I personally have lost several innocent friends and relatives here in Iraq. They were murdered, in 1991, for absolutely no reason. Um Abbass used to make bread, Iraqi bread, so she could earn money to support her three children. She built a small tin house on a vacant plot of land not far away from where I lived. She used to make excellent bread and would send it with her son to my house for a few coins. Every day I got my fresh bread. But one day, someone in your American government decided that her tin house was a legitimate military target and a threat to world security. So you bombed it. Um Abbass and her three children, God bless their souls, were murdered in Baghdad—over eight hundred kilometers away from the war to drive the Iraqi army out of Kuwait! If I knew where she is buried, I would tell her that bread does not taste the same, even after eleven years.

Our neighborhood also had a very young and nice-looking traffic policeman. We used to exchange greetings every time I passed the intersection. Sometimes he kindly turned a blind eye if I ran the stop sign. We were friends, even though we did not know each other's names. He was murdered while he was directing ambulances and fire fighting trucks. He was trying to save the lives of innocent people who were subjected to the most cruel and inhuman air bombardment in the twentieth century. My friend, like the New York police officers who were killed on September 11, was doing his job protecting civilians. The only difference is that the world's greatest government, the U.S.A., killed my friend, while the New York policemen were killed by a few radicals.

The only difference is that the world's greatest government, the U.S.A., killed my friend, while the New York policemen were killed by a few radicals.

Do you people know anything of the horrors of those forty-three days of hell that your government inflicted upon us in 1991? I will need a lot more than forty-three days of crying for my cousin Ahmad, his wife Layla, his sons Kamel and Shehab, and their ten-year-old beautiful girl, Shema. Probably I am fooling myself in believing that they were asleep when the bomb hit their house. I want to believe that they died instantly, without knowing what hit them, else I go crazy. I will need a lot more than forty-three days of crying for the more than four hundred civilians—women, children, and old people—who were incinerated at Alameria civil defense shelter. I will need more than forty-three days to cry for the thousands and thousands of innocent civilians who died in 1991 because of your American terrorist acts against the civilian population of Iraq. And to cry for the hundreds of thousands (if not a million and a half) more who have died because of the U.S.-led sanctions is by far beyond anybody's emotional capability.

Did not your "civilized West" watch the massacre of our civilians on television with jubilation? Did not your "victorious" army march through downtown New York, probably past the World Trade Center, with such rejoicing and fanfare? The best producers in Hollywood could not put on any better show. Naturally, you wanted everyone around the world to watch this spectacular "victory parade" so you beamed it to every TV station in the world. Your government thought that satellite television broadcast was the best way to spread your American values. But this marvelous innovation has turned even more people against your country.

تأمل وزارة الإعلام تسهيل مهمة حامل هذه البطاقة
بصفته الشخصية في حدود ما يسمح به النظام وخلال
المدة المصرح بها.
كما يرجى من حامل البطاقة وضعها في مكان بارز
والإخطار عند فقدها مع مراعاة عدم دخول وتصوير
المنشآت العسكرية والنفطية ومراكز الشرطة إلا بتصريح
مسبق من جهة الإختصاص.

The Ministry of Information Kindly requests from the concerned authorities to facilitate the mission of this card's
bearer within the allowed limits in the set period.
The card should be presented on request and Ministry
should be notified in case of lossing this card.
Entering and filming the restricted areas (such as police
stations, Military Bases , Oil Premises , ... etc) are strictly
prohibited unless prior permission from the concerned authority

For eleven years most of the Arab world has watched through their TV the destruction of Iraq and the hardship inflicted on our people. Naturally, Arab satellite channels devoted more time than the American media to the plight of the Iraqi people. A lot of these satellite channels invited U.S. officials to explain their policy toward Iraq to the Arab masses. I am sorry to say that those idiots did more harm than good to your image. The phone-in response from the Arabs in the West and even Iraqis abroad was so anti-U.S. that it made your officials look truly pathetic.

We also watched as Arab governments were led, like sheep to the slaughterhouse, to join the American coalition against Iraq, believing it would lead to the settlement of the Arab-Israeli conflict. The Americans talked on and on about the return of the Palestinian refugees and exchanging land for peace. But only stupid people believe in American sincerity. After Oslo, Madrid, Camp David—after eleven years of piss talk, or is it peace talk—the Israelis were using F16 fighter planes, helicopter gun ships, and tanks to attack stone-throwing Palestinians. They destroyed hundreds of houses, orchards, schools, and telephone systems—just like your country did in Iraq. Naturally, "civilized America and the West" asked only the Palestinians for restraint. Your free American media freely elected to ignore the plight of the Palestinians; they freely distorted facts; they freely and willfully demonized the Palestinians and Arabs. Yes, you have a free press! But we in the Arab world watched every day on our TV the shelling, the killing, the beating, and the humiliation of women, children, and elderly Palestinians. We also watched the massacres and the ethnic cleansing of Moslems in Bosnia who were supposedly under protection by the NATO forces.

I think Americans need to know that it is the American foreign policy that is the root of the problems you are facing and not Usama bin Laden. To get rid of the Russians from Afghanistan, the American government played the religious game. Since communism was equated with atheism then it was the duty of the Moslems to fight in Afghanistan. The American government created, trained, supplied, supported various organizations for the holy war "Jihad" against the atheist Afghan government. The Afghan-Arabs were the main fighting force in Afghanistan. They included such "freedom fighters," as the Americans called them at that time, like Omar Abdulrahman, Usama bin Laden, Abuhamza al-Musri. Once the Russians were driven out of Afghanistan, those fighters turned their attention to what was happening in the Arab and Moslem countries. Bin Laden resisted the presence of the American forces in the Moslem's holiest places. Naturally, the American and Saudi governments were not happy with him. I think it is foolish to expect him to accept the American presence in the Moslem's holiest places when he spent years fighting to drive the Russians out of Afghanistan. To add insult to injury, bin Laden watched, like the rest of the Arab world, what happened

I think Americans need to know that it is the American foreign policy that is the root of the problems you are facing and not Usama bin Laden.

to Iraq, Sudan, Libya, Lebanon, and Palestine, which further alienated him. This drove him crazy and he soon was transferred from "freedom fighter" to the most wanted "terrorist."

I think it is time for you in the "civilized West" to take an honest look at your own terrorist activities. You are the richest and strongest nation in the world, yet you ceaselessly attack the poorest, weakest, and most primitive nations in the world. You may indeed drive us to the Stone Age … but at what price? You may be able to kill Usama bin Laden, but how many more bin Ladens will be created in the process? Don't forget, we all are going to watch the massacres on our TVs!

> *I think it is time for you in the "civilized West" to take an honest look at your own terrorist activities.*

The late Reverend Martin Luther King Jr. was murdered in your country by a White Anglo Saxon Protestant fanatic, not by a terrorist. But if you believe in the Day of Judgment, you know that Martin Luther King will meet Um Abbass, my cousin Ahmad, Layla, Kamel, Shehab, Shema, and the other millions who are victims of U.S. terrorism. He will remind them that he once warned that America has guided missiles but misguided people. The misguided people didn't like what he said, so they killed him.

Sincerely,

Ghazwan Al-Mukhtar

February 2005

Dear Erica,

I know that it has been a long time since I wrote the "letter to America." A lot of things happened since then, the war and the current occupation, or as they call it "liberation."

One of the most important questions in my mind is "do the American people REALLY want to know what is being done in their name? or are they content to accept what is being dished to them by mainstream media as fact?"

To illustrate my puzzlement is the question of the link between Saddam and Al-Qaeda. The Bush administration kept telling the American public, and the world, that Saddam was connected to the 9/11 [attack]. Years later and after many U.S. congressional investigations and reports denying such facts, more than 50% of the American people still believe that Saddam had something to do with 9/11! These reports are issued by the U.S. Congress, not by a radical writer like Ghazwan.

My trip to the U.S. was cancelled by the organizers "for my safety" because and only because it was reported in the press that I will kill Americans if they attack my country and in the defense of my country! Ending up in Guantanamo was not my idea of visiting the U.S.

Erica, we have suffered such pain and disappointment and sadness that we are numb. We are vegetating rather than living.

Last month the election here was shoved down our throats. All the major parties requested that the election be postponed. This reminds me of a story about Mary Antoinette. She was told that the people did not have bread to eat. She said, "Why don't they eat cake?" We don't have anything and they tell us, here is democracy. Take democracy. What do I do with democracy? Does it allow me to walk across the street without the fear of being kidnapped or being shot at or being mugged? Would democracy feed my children? Would democracy allow me to quench my thirst? The U.S. has not done anything to improve the life of Iraqi people. And that is one of the reasons why you are seeing all those attacks.

Best regards,

Ghazwan Al-Mukhtar
Baghdad, occupied Iraq

Jordan

WHERE	Middle East, northwest of Saudi Arabia
SIZE	92,300 sq km, slightly smaller than Indiana
POPULATION	5,611,202 (July 2004 est.)
INFANT MORTALITY	18.11 deaths/1,000 live births
THE PEOPLE	Arab 98%, Circassian 1%, Armenian 1%
RELIGIONS	Sunni Muslim 92%, Christian 6% (majority Greek Orthodox, but some Greek and Roman Catholics, Syrian Orthodox, Coptic Orthodox, Armenian Orthodox, and Protestant denominations), other 2% (several small Shi'a Muslim and Druze populations) (2001 est.)
LANGUAGES	Arabic (official), English widely understood among upper and middle classes
LITERACY RATE	Total population: 91.3% male: 95.9% female: 86.3% (2003 est.)
GOVERNMENT	Constitutional monarchy
CAPITAL	Amman

NADIA N. SHARABI

JORDAN

39 YEARS OLD, FEMALE, HOUSEWIFE

Dear People of America,

I think this is a very good idea to allow us as Arabs to tell you how we feel regarding the policy of the United States in the Middle East.

First I would like to say I am a Moslem Arab and I am very proud of being so. I was raised in a Moslem family who taught me the basics of my religion, Islam, and how people are equal. And I was taught right from wrong, and how to be honest and faithful. I was taught how God granted us this life to live it peacefully and happily.

I always wanted to go and see the United States of America. It was one of my dreams. Why? Well, because people said it was the country of dreams. You can live there happily, peacefully, and you can do what you like and you can make your dreams come true.

I was sixteen years old when I first went to San Diego, California, as an American Field Service (A.F.S.) student. This program was to allow students from all over the world to share their experiences with different students from other countries and to let American students learn about other students' cultures. My A.F.S. year was a good one. I learned many things and I learned how to depend on myself. I also learned how American

people respect you for who you are, and they listen to what you say. They also give you the right to be yourself, and express yourself. The American people are very friendly, they like to help, and they care for you. Once I was invited to a church for the black community, and their priest mentioned that I came from the country Jordan, near the River of Jordan, and many people welcomed me and were pleased to see me.

I also remember in my high school (Patrick Henry High School) how teachers presented me in class to other students and always offered to help me if I needed anything. Whenever I was invited to a place, people would show their interest to hear about my country and our late King Hussein. I went to Atlanta this last January to visit my sister, and I was happy to let my children see the United States, which they loved very much.

Over the last few years, the situation in the Middle East has become very critical, especially with the Israeli/Palestinian problem. To our beliefs, and if we go back to history, it is very well known that Palestine was occupied by Israel in 1948 (with the help of Great Britain), and then was fully occupied in 1967. Thousands of Palestinians were forced to leave their homes and lands that were taken by Israel by force. My whole family was forced to leave their homes in Palestine. When I was a child I always saw my dear parents crying whenever they watched the news, and now, as a grownup, I understand the sadness they feel about their homeland Palestine.

My father was one of the people who left only with a jacket on his back. He left all his school and university certificates and his trophies that he won for his excellence in sports. My father was still unmarried when he was forced to leave Palestine, his home and country. We could see the sadness in his eyes whenever he spoke about how awful it was to leave his home. I also remember once when we were going to Jerusalem for the wedding of my cousin. We were crossing the bridge from Jordan to Jericho, and my father cried, because it was the first time he went back to visit Palestine after he was forced to leave. He could not stand the idea of Israelis being there. And that was the last time my father visited Palestine. "It was a devastating disaster," my father always says, having to leave your home and country by force. It is cruel and unfair.

"It was a devastating disaster," my father always says, having to leave your home and country by force. It is cruel and unfair.

My mother always mentions to us how their furniture was stolen and her beautiful piano was stolen too, and her father kept looking for it until he finally bought another one for her. Even now our relatives can't come and visit us from Palestine, although it is only one hour drive by car. But because of the Israelis and their checkpoints, they make it cruel and hard for anyone to leave or visit. I feel very sad deep inside, how the Israelis are treating the Palestinians and how they have treated my family. I feel worried and unhappy. Why can't the Palestinians live freely, happily, and peacefully? Let them go on with their lives and be a better nation. Give them back their lands. Why can't they be respected and treated well? We are humans, after all. The occupation made millions of Palestinians and Arabs suffer.

The many great ideas about the United States that I had when I was an A.F.S. student have changed now because of all the unfair foreign policy the United States is using, especially with the Palestinians.

The Americans call the Palestinians who defend their land and fight for their lives "terrorists." Well, it's their land and they want to kick the Israeli invaders out of Palestine. The Israelis are invaders; they stole Palestine by force, but they say it's their right to defend themselves in an other peoples' country. This is unfair.

What the U.S. is saying now is unfair and there is no justice. They say the Palestinians are terrorists; we say and believe that the U.S. policy towards the Palestinians is terrorism itself. This policy is not clean and is not fair. It's against religion.

We as Arabs know and believe that the Palestinians have the right to defend their homeland and to live in peace. The Israelis must go out of Palestine. Why do the American people have the right to live peacefully, happily, and respectfully? What about us, the Arab Palestinians? Where are our rights? Why does the United States give itself the right to judge other people the way it wants? This is unfair.

The United States may be a great country now, but history changes—and, by the lapse of days, people change too, and there will be another great country.

All I ask from you, dear People of America, is to be fair; let there be peace on Earth. "It's a small world, after all." Read and you will understand history in our region and how Palestine was stolen from us.

Long ago I was taught that the United States was great and

Long ago I was taught that the United States was great and beautiful, but now my children are not taught the same. They are taught that the United States of America is unfair and it is the reason of our crises in the Middle East.

beautiful, but now my children are not taught the same. They are taught that the United States of America is unfair and it is the reason of our crises in the Middle East.

Save yourself, America; keep your good beliefs; leave evil and try to regain the confidence of the world. People are fighting against your policy with their ideas and money. They are raising a generation to hate you. The United States of America is stealing from us the dream of living happily in peace, and is killing our hope in life. Where is justice, America? Come on, give us the right to live like you American people. Let us work on loving, sharing, and building ourselves on hope and a bright future. Leave the Palestinian children, Iraqi children, and Moslem children to live in peace and happiness. It is God who grants life, not you.

Thank you for reading my letter. May God lead us the right way.

Nadia

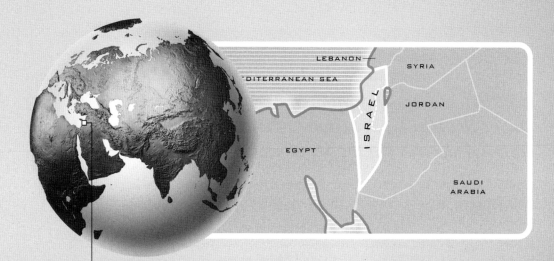

ISRAEL

WHERE	Middle East, bordering the Mediterranean Sea, between Egypt and Lebanon
SIZE	20,770 sq km, slightly smaller than New Jersey
POPULATION	6,199,008
INFANT MORTALITY	7.21 deaths/1,000 live births (2004 est.)
THE PEOPLE	Jewish 80.1% (Europe/America-born 32.1%, Israel-born 20.8%, Africa-born 14.6%, Asia-born 12.6%), non-Jewish 19.9% (mostly Arab)
RELIGIONS	Jewish 80.1%, Muslim 14.6% (mostly Sunni Muslim), Christian 2.1%, other 3.2%
LANGUAGES	Hebrew (official), Arabic used officially for Arab minority, English most commonly used foreign language
LITERACY RATE	Total population: 95.4% male: 97.3% female: 93.6% (2003 est.)
GOVERNMENT	Parliamentary democracy
CAPITAL	Jerusalem. *Note*: Israel proclaimed Jerusalem as its capital in 1950, but the US, like nearly all other countries, maintains its Embassy in Tel Aviv.

ASSAF ORON

ISRAEL

37 YEARS OLD, MALE, REFUSNIK, BIOTECH STARTUP
MANAGER, PHD STUDENT IN STATISTICS

Dear People of America,

We learn in history about processes of barbarization, when a developed
civilization gives way and falls apart. It is not pleasant to witness such a
process happening in another land. But it is a grueling, stomach-turning
experience to live through it. It has been happening to me over the past
several years, here in the Holy Land. Now, in the darkness, my society
is shrugging off open thought, diversity, creativity, tolerance, rationality,
morality—as if they were excess baggage. As I write, my nation sends
its young and spends immense resources in order to murder and starve
innocents, to destroy and loot property, with the clear knowledge that
some of us will be cruelly murdered in revenge for these acts. I feel like a
stranger, in exile in my own land. The air itself has become too foul and
heavy to breathe.

I know I'm taking it too personally. After all, I can probably keep myself
out of trouble if I want to. I have a good job. I have two young sons and
a wife, whom I adore and love, but my family life is being eroded by my
involvement. I am losing weight. Even though my daily life still passes
in relative prosperity and freedom, I look as if I'm under siege like the

Palestinians, or as if one of my relatives has fallen victim to the cycle of violence. My wife has become used to going to sleep alone, seeing the silhouette of my back against the flickering computer screen, consumed by the endless reports and pleas for help. See, I cannot afford to take it personally, but I can't help it. What would you have done in my place? And what does it have to do with you Americans?

Perhaps I should start by offering you a glimpse into the mechanism of our self-destruction.

I saw Gaza for the first time in 1985, when during infantry basic training we had to perform 'security duties' there from time to time. I have a couple of memory flashes. A night ride in an army bus, perhaps my first ride into Gaza. All the towns were under the permanent night curfew. The sidewalks were strange, made of rough concrete. Everything looked poor and beat-up. We suddenly stopped, and our commanders ran out into the street. Apparently some young guys had broken curfew, and our commanders caught them and started beating them. It wasn't too brutal, but I was very confused. It wasn't the type of behavior I'd learned to expect from my commanders. Not that I was judging them; but I didn't get into too many fights during my teenage years, and when I did I usually lost. What was going on? Was I up to the task? Would I need to learn this stuff?

Another time, our company was sitting in a bus outside the Military Government headquarters in Rafah, waiting to be assigned. One of the soldiers, a troublemaker who had a tough time keeping up with basic training, found his calling. As a Palestinian man was walking by the bus, this soldier stuck his head out of the bus window and spat on the man, accompanying the act with a long racist curse. Apparently, this soldier knew what was going on, and was much more ready for the job than I was. But as my three years of service went by I caught up…

Only after my service was over, did I understand how wrong it all was. Gradually I began to see the big picture. I've learned to recognize the corruption that permeates all of our public life, top to bottom, from the local level to the national level. The word "corruption" brings to mind images of money exchanging hands in back rooms. Though this also happens here, it's not what I'm talking about. The corruption in Israel is about having power without any minimal sense of responsibility. Without any acknowledgement that there are rules governing what they may or may not do. This, of course, includes the rules of cause and effect.

I've learned to recognize the corruption that permeates all of our public life, top to bottom, from the local level to the national level.

I don't really know where this culture came from, but I know its implications all too well. The public, conditioned to think that "this is the way democracy works" lets politicians get away with anything—scandals, bloody catastrophes, even personal theft—without losing popularity. On the other hand, when once in a blue moon a different type of politician emerges, one who attempts to address and resolve the real problems, something fascinating occurs: he draws huge waves of resentment for treading on unfamiliar ground and for "breaking all the rules" and is summarily dismissed. The classic, extreme example is Yitzhak Rabin's isolation and eventual assassination in 1995.

This perverse culture is the reason why I was sent to Gaza in 1985. And again in 1987, and again in 1993 (already a reservist), and again in 1997 (after we had supposedly "moved out of Gaza"). And even more time in the West Bank throughout the years. This is why, in between Gaza's packed cities and refugee camps (and all over the hills of the West Bank), sit thousands of Israelis who were lured there by messianic dreams or (more often) by huge government subsidies. They live on land that was never made part of Israel. Yet, they receive the best infrastructure and public services Israel can offer (while most other Israeli citizens have to make do with barely mediocre services). All around them are hundreds of thousands of Palestinians with no infrastructure, no services, no rights, and no future.

What do you Americans have to do with it? Like me with my tax money and my army service, you too have helped finance this madness.

What do you Americans have to do with it? Like me with my tax money and my army service, you too have helped finance this madness. My government counts on your immense contributions to its budget, in public and private money. Without your support, this universe of corruption called "the Occupation of the West Bank and the Gaza Strip" could not have flourished and survived for so long.

At some point, your government tried to deduct settlement-related investments from the U.S. aid money, but these have no separate clause in the Israeli budget. Seasoned white-collar criminals, the involved officials and politicians have camouflaged these immense expenditures in the budgets of all government and para-government institutions. You paid for it, whether you liked it or not. You paid for creating a full-fledged Apartheid regime in East Jerusalem, the West

You paid for creating a full-fledged Apartheid regime in East Jerusalem, the West Bank, and Gaza.

Bank, and Gaza. And through your defense budget aid, you paid to send me there as a soldier and enforce this regime. Only in fall 2000, after I became a father and witnessed the peace process collapse, did I have the courage to step out of line and refuse to join in these crimes. For this I'm being branded as "the enemy of the people" by most Jews around me and by many Jews abroad.

Why did you help fund our criminal abuse of the Occupied Territories, and our wicked treatment of their inhabitants? Look, I'm not blaming you for it all. Of course it was our decision to corrupt our society, it is my governments who have pursued these insane settlements and oppression policies. But why did you help us do it? Why are you still helping us go down the drain? Are political interests driving you? It would seem that the cool-headed interest of any world power would be to see quiet and good relationships among this volatile region's peoples. So why?

Dear Americans! Like most Palestinians, like most Israelis, your attitude to this conflict is blinded by your emotions. You have clear, strong emotions toward both sides. On one side, the Palestinians–Arabs (not a likeable ethnicity in the U.S. since September 11, so I gather), and some of them keep perpetrating these heinous terror attacks. On the other side, the Israelis, your Precious Ones, the apples of your eyes, so democratic and

Western and modern. Not a difficult choice, is it? Your adoring eyes fail to see the blatant corruption, the thirty-five-year Apartheid, the no-less-heinous nature of our army's "policies" and "operations" (perpetrated not by extremist militants, but by our official U.S.-sponsored troops). You seem to forget that all this time we have been controlling the Palestinians' life, not vice versa, and therefore holding us accountable and ending this domination must be the first unconditional step towards any resolution.

No, you just close your eyes, and provide us with full blanket coverage against all those Anti-Semites (what do you know, even the Danes are Anti-Semites now). You love us with the unconditional love that a parent loves a child. The fact is that you are spoiling us (or rather, our government) rotten against everyone's good. You have turned us into the rotten spoiled brat of the neighborhood. You have shielded us for so long from paying for the consequences of our actions, that now we find ourselves paying with compound interest and we don't even understand why. What's worse, even you still don't understand.

In April 2002, at the height of our army's re-occupation offensive into Palestinian cities, Secretary Powell stormed in here, apparently to calm things down, but immediately turned to blame the Palestinians for everything, and left as quickly as he arrived. What message did your disastrous visit convey to the Palestinians, Secretary Powell? You let them understand that they are alone in the world, deserted to their fate at Israel's mercy. You let them understand that if they want freedom, they would have to fight for it even more cruelly than before. That was your contribution to quiet in our region, Secretary Powell.

Dear Americans, I am honored by your friendship. In the name of this friendship, please open up your eyes and see our government and political institutions for what they are—utterly corrupt bodies that befit the worst regimes.

Some wise Israelis and American Jews have noticed this corruption quite a while ago, and therefore have set up numerous funds and NGO's that honestly work to better the lives of Israelis and Palestinians in this land. If you want to give, give to them. Please do not give our Establishment (in its many disguises) a single penny.

I don't want to mislead you; my opinions represent a minority in Israel. But truth, life, and basic human rights are not matters for majority decision. Nor are the Commandments: thou shalt not steal, thou shalt not murder.

Being in a small minority, I cannot stop my government. I can't stop them from playing this lopsided ping-pong game of carnage, all the way to its hideous conclusion.

But you can.

Please stop them. Please.

Thanks in advance,

Assaf

IRAN

WHERE	Middle East, bordering the Gulf of Oman, the Persian Gulf, and the Caspian Sea, between Iraq and Pakistan
SIZE	1.648 million sq km, slightly larger than Alaska
POPULATION	69,018,924 (July 2004 est.)
INFANT MORTALITY	42.86 deaths/1,000 live births
THE PEOPLE	Persian 51%, Azeri 24%, Gilaki and Mazandarani 8%, Kurd 7%, Arab 3%, Lur 2%, Baloch 2%, Turkmen 2%, other 1%
RELIGIONS	Shi'a Muslim 89%, Sunni Muslim 10%, Zoroastrian, Jewish, Christian, and Baha'i 1%
LANGUAGES	Persian and Persian dialects 58%, Turkic and Turkic dialects 26%, Kurdish 9%, Luri 2%, Balochi 1%, Arabic 1%, Turkish 1%, other 2%
LITERACY RATE	Total population: 79.4% male: 85.6% female: 73% (2003 est.)
GOVERNMENT	Theocratic republic
CAPITAL	Tehran

Mojgan Farahmand

Iran

35 years old, female, midwife

Dear People of America,

My name is Mojgan. I am an Iranian woman, age thirty-five. I live in Tehran, (capital city of Iran) but I was born in Kerman that is located by the salt desert. I am a midwife and I work in a clinic every day. I love my job.

I have many pen pals from all over the world. I like all of them very much, but I mostly enjoy getting letters from the U.S.A. All of the world knows us as big enemies, but I don't think so. I think we don't know each other very well. I want to know you better. I have eleven American pen pals. They all are very good friends, interesting and honest, but very different. It amazes me how different they all are.

I have two sons. I am helping my children know other countries and other people via my pen pals. I noticed that nearly for all of us, our children are the most important things in our life. We all try to do our best for them. We want them to have everything that they want and like. We all work hard for it. I believe we can buy nearly everything that they need, but we can't buy for our children "LOVE" and "LIKE". I think they must learn these things from us. If they don't learn from us how to like and love others, they can't like and love others. Have you ever seen the people that

73

apparently have everything but they don't feel happiness? Why? I think because they don't know how to like and love others and even themselves. I talk to my children about my love for my American pen pals every night when we are eating our dinner. This teaches them to love people from all different places and cultures.

I talk to my children about my love for my American pen pals every night when we are eating our dinner. This teaches them to love people from all different places and cultures.

In many of our letters we wrote about differences of our cultures and our political views. David (one of my pen pals) always told me that we are terrorists. I tried to explain to him my views, but he thought I'm influenced by my government. Of course I know we have many mistakes in our past, but I can't understand why David couldn't understand that it is not related to my love for my country. For all of us, our country is like our mother. We always love our own mothers. We never love any one else's mother, because for example she is more beautiful or more modern. To me Iran is like my mother, and I love it with all of its mistakes. Unfortunately, David couldn't understand it. He was angry with me and even he didn't write me for a long time, but at last again he wrote me. Since then we have learned that we can be good friends even if we have different views and ideas.

Tommy is my other American pen pal. Our friendship is a little strange! The first time he wrote to me I replied to him at once. But after a few times he didn't write me. But still I always send him the Iranian poems and articles that I usually send to my other pen pals. He only replies me with one or two words! For example he writes "good" or "interesting'" or "OK'" and, of course, "cool!" One night I was talking about Tommy with my children. Shervin (my first son) asked me, "Maman! Why do you continue to write him?" I replied, "Because he is my friend and I like him." Shervin said, "I'm not sure, because he is an American and they don't like us." I was very sad for it, but didn't say anything. Two weeks later I had some difficulties with my mailbox, so I couldn't write to my pen pals for one week. One evening Shervin and I were in an Internet cafe for checking my emails. I had many emails. One of them was from Tommy. He only wrote: "Where are you?" I showed it to Shervin and said, "Shervin, read it. It shows that Tommy likes us. Tommy is an American, but he likes us. Friendship is not related to these things." Shervin smiled and I was sure that I won't have to buy him "LOVE" and "LIKE."

And Mark! He has changed all of my views about Americans. He is a wonderful person and a great friend. He is an artist, forty years old, married without children. I had heard: "Americans are lazy people that don't work!" But from Mark, I have learned that Americans are the people that work hard and love their jobs. I had heard: "Americans are not informed about their country and their history. For them the most important thing is pop music!" But from Mark I have learned that Americans are very informed. Mark's information about everything always amazes me. I had heard: "They don't like their family! They are not tied to their wives!" But from Mark, I have learned it is not true at all. In all of Mark's letters I can see and feel his love for his family, especially to his wife and parents. I had heard: "Americans have a modern and busy life and they don't know their neighbors!" But from Mark I have learned that he knows all of his neighbors. In fact it is me who doesn't know most of my nieghbors! I had heard: "Americans are not religious and they are not interested in religions." But it's always interesting for me that my American friend Mark has an Iranian friend (me) that isn't religious at all and I have an American pen pal that is very interested and informed in religions! I had heard: "Americans don't like us!" I don't know if Mark likes me! But I see in all of his letters he respects me. Mark changed all of my views. I don't know if I have been successful as much as him. I don't know if I could change his views about Iranians. I know like me, he has heard many things about us that are not true. I don't know if I could change his views. The only thing that I'm sure about is that we are good friends though he is an American and I am an Iranian.

To me friendship is very valuable. I don't want to be friends with my pen pals for a short time. I wish for a day when we can send each other pictures of our grandchildren.

Now to me, America is Mark! I see America through Mark's eyes. I have never seen any country except Iran. But I imagine America is a very beautiful and nice country with kind and friendly people, because Mark's eyes say it to me.

To me friendship is very valuable. I don't want to be friends with my pen pals for a short time. I wish for a day when we can send each other pictures of our grandchildren. I do know that my American friends

Our happiness, our sorrow, our thoughts, our dreams, our problems and difficulties, and even our mistakes are very alike.

and I rarely have a vivid eye-to-eye view, but I hope our children could see each other more easily than us, and of course in a better world.

The most beautiful and important thing that I have learned from these experiences is that we all are very similar. Our happiness, our sorrow, our thoughts, our dreams, our problems and difficulties, and even our mistakes are very alike. Of course, it has a simple reason! Because we all are human!

Not more, not less, only human!

Not Angel, not Devil, only human!

What a simple but very beautiful reality! Sometimes some of us forget it!

Maybe we have many differences, but always friendship rules above all. Don't you think so, my American friends?

Your friend,

Mojgan

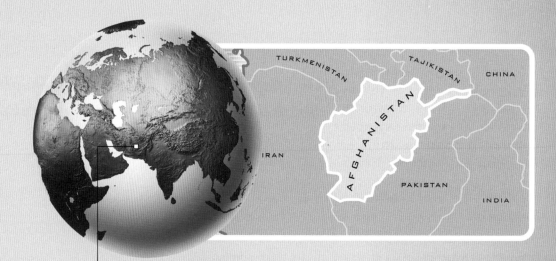

Afghanistan

WHERE	Southern Asia, north and west of Pakistan, east of Iran
SIZE	647,500 sq km, slightly smaller than Texas
POPULATION	28,513,677 (July 2004 est.)
INFANT MORTALITY	165.96 deaths/1,000 live births (2004 est.)
THE PEOPLE	Pashtun 42%, Tajik 27%, Hazara 9%, Uzbek 9%, Aimak 4%, Turkmen 3%, Baloch 2%, other 4%
RELIGIONS	Sunni Muslim 80%, Shi'a Muslim 19%, other 1%
LANGUAGES	Afghan Persian (Dari) 50%, Pashtu (official) 35%, Turkic languages (primarily Uzbek and Turkmen) 11%, 30 minor languages (primarily Balochi and Pashai) 4%, much bilingualism
LITERACY RATE	Total population: 36% male: 51% female: 21%
GOVERNMENT	Transitional
CAPITAL	Kabul

Asad Nasir

Afghanistan

24 years old, male, medical student

Dear People of America,

My name is Asad Nasir and I am a twenty-four-year-old, male Afghani medical student in Pakistan. I would like to tell you something about your country and about the influence you have had on my life and lifestyle.

At first the image that I had of America was what I saw in the movies, and since only action movies were commercially successful for the distributors, I saw lots of them, and thought that America must be a very dangerous place to live indeed. Then, my father visited America personally and he was more than impressed, so much so that he decided that maybe one day we should live there. But it was not until the communist coup d'etat and the Mujahiddin resistance that he gave it a serious consideration. Now, almost thirty years after his first visit, he is a U.S. citizen, and his children—me included—are waiting to get their visas and settle in this country, which by some is called the land of the dreams.

I was eleven in Kabul, Afghanistan, and I remember pretty vividly what it was like. A typical day would begin very early, as early as 7 a.m.; we did not know what sleeping-in felt like. Breakfast was a family affair, with everybody dashing off to school or work. I remember my own school very

Now here is an interesting concept: America thinks (or should I say justifies itself to think) that whatever action America takes to defend its interests is 100% legal, while the same action by other countries is termed aggression or supporting terror or conducting state-terrorism.

well, a nice place (but then it was a poor school and the building could not compare to even a private house these days when it comes to facilities like running water and gas and all). Having said this, Kabul was growing rapidly, new buildings were being erected, and roads built. The people were fiercely independent and patriotic, the hatred for Russians (we had Russians at that time in our country) was instilled in everybody's heart, and in spite of them being nice toward us, they always received glares and abuses.

The era of Mujahiddin (1993 to 1997) was that of terror. People being kidnapped, houses looted, really awful. Our own home was looted. My dad was kidnapped and released after ransom. So all I remember from this time period is fear and hatred. The Taliban era (1997 to 2001) was that of oppression and rage, and all I can say about it is that thank God it is over.

Throughout the 1980s and early 1990s, America aided the Mujahiddin. The details of this are still a secret, or at least that is what I think. I heard claims of $5 billion being spent on what some people called operation Cyclone. How much of this is a fact and how much a figment of imagination of people, I am not a judge of, but I did see the fragments of Russian airplanes that were hit by Stinger missiles by the Mujahiddin, and I did hear commanders discussing prices like $1 million for a single stinger missile being offered by the Americans, once they realized the war was over and that these could cause a security threat to America.

Now here is an interesting concept: America thinks (or should I say justifies itself to think) that whatever action America takes to defend its interests is 100% legal while the same action by other countries is termed aggression or supporting terror or conducting state-terrorism.

I cannot possibly refrain from mentioning September 11 and the things that happened afterwards. You cannot imagine how happy the people of Afghanistan are that the Taliban are no more, I being one of them. But, I personally know so many people who lost dear ones to the relentless American bombing, and I equally feel sorry for the American soldiers who were unfamiliar with the guerrilla tactics that Afghan people have become so used to, and lost their lives. Of course the American military machine is superior and eventually they achieve victories, but to be honest, there are bad things that happen in war that the American people do not know about. I am not a specialist in ethics or warfare, but the treatment of the Al-Qaida or Taliban prisoners was indeed cruel. I do believe this is a double standard.

So how has this all affected me? Well, my dad had his car, offices, and other assets confiscated and he was on a wanted list by the Taliban, all because he was uncle to a person who had financial dealings with the former regime. But now he can go to his country as a free man; in fact, that is what he exactly did a few days ago. I myself can go back after my education is complete, while before it was unimaginable to live with the strict rules and regulations of the Taliban.

There are some other effects that you the Americans have had on me. A few years ago, the favorite hangout for us used to be the local park or the market, but now it is either KFC or the McDonalds or Dunkin Donuts. We are more enthusiastic about the Oscars then the local football championships. Our favorite Website for information is CNN.com or Yahoo. Our favorite sportswear is Nike, and we have started spelling colour as color, the American way. I am not much alarmed by this personally as I am not against the positive effects your culture is having on us, but there are some things that have been done in our own way for ages, and the American way just does not seem to work.

We cannot begin to understand how a small country like Israel is so dear to America that it risks severing its relation to its Arab allies and will not consider scolding Israel for its nasty actions.

For example, my dad's best friend married an American lady against his parent's wishes. In time, he was so Americanized and did not care to practice the traditions of his past in Afghanistan. He stopped contacting his parents and they eventually passed away. He broke up with his wife some years later and he came back looking for a new person to spend his life with. He was adamant that this time, it should be a traditional marriage, and the person should be eastern in her thinking and character. I met him when he came back, and he had changed so much that he no longer fitted as a member of our society; everything he did or said was alien to us, and maybe everything we did or said was awkward for him.

There are some aspects of your country that I absolutely dislike, or if I may use the word hate, I would not be much wrong. The

Muslim people, me included, can never ever forgive America for its policy towards the Palestinians. We cannot begin to understand how a small country like Israel is so dear to America that it risks severing its relation to its Arab allies and will not consider scolding Israel for its nasty actions. How can a small country hold the entire American Middle East policy hostage, and make it do whatever it wants? History is a very unforgiving thing and you may have to pay dearly for the unequal behavior toward the Middle East.

I hate how people are mistreated at arriving at the American airports from the Asian region, as if they were livestock and not humans. I hate how roughly we are spoken to by the counselors in the American embassies. The one lady that I spoke to was a prime example of how Cleopatra must have treated her slaves. I personally do not like the fact that to meet up with my family in the U.S., I would have to wait twenty-seven months for my application to become due. To be honest, the American embassies now have become impenetrable fortresses.

Finally, I would like to advise you, the people of America, that whenever you implement some new policy or some new tactic on the rest of the world, just take two minutes, imagine yourself in my place, and think whether you would like this thing to be done to you or not, for I believe it is the Bible that says do unto others …

With this I say good bye and wish you all the best.

Asad Nasir

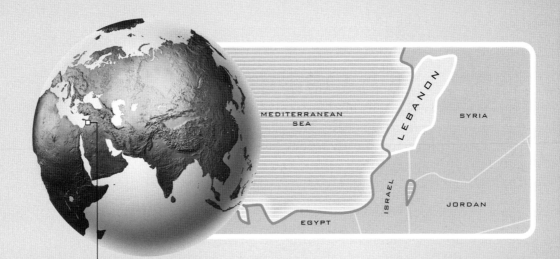

Lebanon

WHERE	Middle East, bordering the Mediterranean Sea, between Israel and Syria
SIZE	10,400 sq km, about 0.7 times the size of Connecticut
POPULATION	3,777,218 (July 2004 est.)
INFANT MORTALITY	25.48 deaths/1,000 live births
THE PEOPLE	Arab 95%, Armenian 4%, other 1%
RELIGIONS	Muslim 70% (including Shi'a, Sunni, Druze, Isma'ilite, Alawite or Nusayri), Christian 30% (including Orthodox Christian, Catholic, Protestant), Jewish NEGL 1%
LANGUAGES	Arabic (official), French, English, Armenian
LITERACY RATE	Total population: 87.4% male: 93.1% female: 82.2% (2003 est.)
GOVERNMENT	Republic
CAPITAL	Beirut

HALA AHMADIEH

LEBANON

19 YEARS OLD, FEMALE, MEDICAL STUDENT

Dear People of America,

How could you be so oblivious to what's going on? You fear us because you don't understand us. We are not the camel-riding desert nomads you think we are. We're people just like you with needs, hopes, fears, wishes, and ambitions. You depict us as villains and terrorists in your movies, but you don't know many important things about us.

In my land, there's a great tendency for people to help each other. It is our duty to help those in need and to be close to people we love and care about. Here I am a member of the Red Cross youth section. I go help kids and old people. I learned to like helping people from my family and some of my friends.

It is rare to live alone here in Lebanon. The family relationship is very tight and your family keeps caring for you even when you are old. Here it is easy to find true friendship, while as I was told in America there is no such thing as true friendship. Or that it is very rare. I have friends like Houda, Marwan, Samar, Tarek, Nadim, Abdallah, Faysal, Hamze, Hadeel, Zeina, Omar, and many others. We go out all as a group, do everything together and we always thank God that we are really close. We go out to the cinema, study together, we grew up together, we laugh a lot. Hadeel

I think in America all you do is work many hours a day, missing important moments that you could spend with your family.

and Hamze went to America three years ago and they have told us that it's not similar to have true friends in America. They felt lonely in your land. I think in America all you do is work many hours a day, missing important moments that you could spend with your family. I don't know, is this a better way to live? In Lebanon, our family bond makes us miss many opportunities. For example, my parents don't want me to travel to continue my studies somewhere else because they want me to be near to them. I am in the university and I want to go into medicine next year but I can't afford continuing in the American University in Beirut.

We do have problems in the Middle East, anyone could see that. It is your responsibility as a powerful nation to interfere, but you should understand that you are not being objective in dealing with the problems. When I watch CNN, I see Arabs viewed as terrorists and as very bad people, but believe me, this is not the case. If only you could watch the news and see what Israeli people are doing to Arabs! But your CNN doesn't show that. Many people have been killed in a brutal way and many have lost their families. Yet you Americans still help the Israelis and never try to understand the Arabs. We too have lived several years suffering from terrorist acts, especially what was happening in the south of Lebanon. But do you care? You never try to stop Israel from doing that. I wonder why.

Israelis are just killing people and they don't care. I just hate Israel! How could I consider your government any good when you are helping all these Israelis to commit their crimes? What Israeli people are doing is horrible and I really hope that one day they will be punished for what they are doing. Consider yourself in the Palestinian people's place … what could you do?

Concerning what happened on September 11; I felt really sorry for what happened. It is a cruel act and those people responsible for doing it should be punished. When I was watching on TV what was happening I was really sad because this is a tragic event and those who were involved in doing it are insane. But not all extremists are insane. Some of the Muslims I know are extremist, but this is the way they grew up, and I think that everyone has the right to live in the way they like. You shouldn't hate them. It is a way of life. I have a friend who's close to me and he's extreme Muslim and he is so nice, so kind. He offers help whenever needed. He has a strong faith in God and believes he has to do jihad in order to live freely—and I guess this is right. Muslim extremists are not dangerous, believe me, if you try to understand them. I used to have this belief about them too, but if you get closer and look at the way they think, you'll notice that they are good and kind and not cruel. The people who committed the terrorists attacks were crazy, but you can't say that all Muslims are the same. I hope that you understand what I mean.

You consider us cruel people, but please stop with stereotypes and suspicions of us. We are all human beings like you. I am a person who would ask for peace all over the world, and I am sure that by communication we could all live peacefully and won't have to live in fear. The children want us to live peacefully; we should all think of them.

I hope that you are not shocked by what I am telling you. You asked me to be honest and that's what I am trying to do. I would like to end with only one thing: "Give peace a chance."

Hala

AFRICA

GHANA

NIGERIA

MOROCCO

ZIMBABWE

EGYPT

NIGER

CAMEROON

MALI

M. Brecke

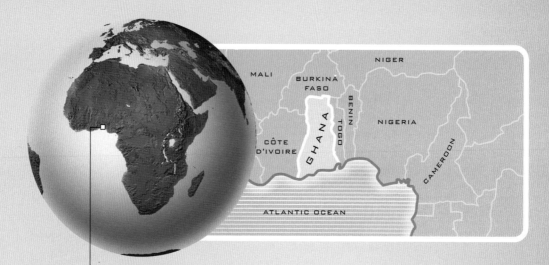

GHANA

WHERE	Western Africa, bordering the Gulf of Guinea, between Cote d'Ivoire and Togo
SIZE	239,460 sq km, slightly smaller than Oregon
POPULATION	20,757,032 *Note*: estimates for this country explicitly take into account the effects of excess mortality due to AIDS (July 2004 est.)
INFANT MORTALITY	52.22 deaths/1,000 live births
THE PEOPLE	Black African 98.5% (major tribes—Akan 44%, Moshi-Dagomba 16%, Ewe 13%, Ga 8%, Gurma 3%, Yoruba 1%), European and other 1.5%
RELIGIONS	Christian 63%, Indigenous beliefs 21%, Muslim 16%
LANGUAGES	English (official), African languages (including Akan, Moshi-Dagomba, Ewe, and Ga)
LITERACY RATE	Total population: 74.8% (2003 est.) male: 82.7% female: 67.1%
GOVERNMENT	Constitutional democracy
CAPITAL	Accra

CHRIS ASHIE-MENSAH

GHANA

29 YEARS OLD, MALE, BANKER

Dear People of America,

Greetings from Ghana! Recently, I watched a documentary on Ghana Television (GTV). The film showed people from West Africa crossing the Sahara Desert on foot in search of greener pastures abroad. In the film you would see the skulls and carcasses of those who got lost in the desert. Some died through thirst and hunger whilst others were eaten by wild animals. Where were all these people going? Most of them were migrating to America through Europe.

Kofi, who was fortunate to reach Europe, was asked why he took such a great risk. "I cannot make a living in my country. I must find work to care for myself and family," he stated.

These are but few of the people who throng daily at the American Embassy in Ghana looking for visas to your country even when they are not qualified. When all else fails, they take risky steps to get to the shores of America no matter the cost.

There are several reasons why Ghanaians want to reach America even if that will cost them their own lives or the lives of their loved ones. We are of the opinion that anything American is a good thing. Ghana

I advise you to adopt a few poor countries every year and bring them up. There is an adage in our local parlance that states: 'Let your neighbor be satisfied and your peace is assured.'

is a poor country. It is mostly due to the corruption of our government. Over half of our population is living below the poverty line. The rural folks hardly have clean water, access to electricity, or good roads. Many cannot afford one square meal a day. You need to visit our countryside to understand what it really means to be poor. However, Ghana has good brains that can be tapped by your country. So as long as Ghanaians must live, come what may, you should expect a troop of us to your country.

Due to the failure of our politicians to properly govern our country, soldiers mostly take over through the barrels of guns. Economic instability, moral decay, and corruption at the highest level have always been the result. During the 1979 coup in Ghana, I had to flee our home with my parents because we were near the army barracks and bullets were flying over our heads. I saw people gunned down just like we normally see in your cowboys' films and movies. People were stripped naked and brutalized in the streets of Accra. A horrible sight!

The beauty of any culture lies in its power to unite the people. Over the years that beauty has eluded the Ghanaian people. We are left with greed and avarice, backbiting, hatred, and selfishness. One cultural practice that has seriously eaten into the very fiber of our society is the notion that "the big man does no wrong." This notion has permeated the political atmosphere, the business entity, and the home. This makes it very difficult to speak up in our country—we have no way to tell the "boss" when he goes wrong. In America, everyone has the freedom to speak out against corruption.

You Americans are generally God-fearing people just like our people. The blessings that we have received both materially and spiritually from American Christians cannot be overemphasized. In Ghana, Christianity was handed to us from our colonial masters. Ghanaians are so enthused about America that we have even "Americanized" our way of worship. Ghanaians are of the opinion that anything American is a good thing.

The strength of your country lies in one fact: American people are proud of their country. You love your country. Even naturalized Americans are simply proud of their citizenship. I am yet to come across an American who will talk evil of your great nation. About ten years ago, I went to VALCO, an American company owned by Kaiser to solicit for business. The officer-in-charge, an American, told me: "My country is the greatest importer and exporter of everything on earth. We don't need your services." This man is very proud of his country. Can that be said of Ghanaians? No. If we do not like our country, how can we stay in it? Honestly speaking, I want to come to your country to pursue a course of study in business management and marketing. Ghanaians must learn to be hardworking just like your people.

Yours is a prosperous and great nation. God has endowed you with all that it takes to make a nation happy.

Yours is a prosperous and great nation. God has endowed you with all that it takes to make a nation happy. Even the advanced countries look up to you for success. But not all want to enjoy in your success. Many of us think you are too powerful. Others say your pride as a successful nation has gone beyond bounds. The American currency is still the most powerful and most favoured. The fear that your country will rule the world some day is the main cause of the hatred we see against this great nation. But why should you expect love from all people? In fact, the hatred is based on mere perception and not the reality. Americans are generous people. But your generosity is frowned upon by those who think it is just a camouflage—an attempt to enslave or colonize other countries. Hatred for your people might have also stemmed from the religious beliefs of other nationals who feel threatened.

But your generosity is frowned upon by those who think it is just a camouflage—an attempt to enslave or colonize other countries.

Your country will continue to be great, but on your way, do not step on innocent toes. Be very genuine in your dealings with other nations, especially the disadvantaged. I advise you to adopt a few poor countries every year and bring them up. There is an adage in our local parlance that states: "Let your neighbour be satisfied and your peace is assured." Encourage your people to adopt families of other nations, especially Africans who are less privileged. When your help to others is perceived as genuine, the hatred for your country will assuage.

I want to take this great opportunity to wish you all well as you repair the destruction of terrorism, especially the September 11, 2001, calamity. Ghanaians all mourn with you.

Your bosom friend,

Chris

M. Brecke

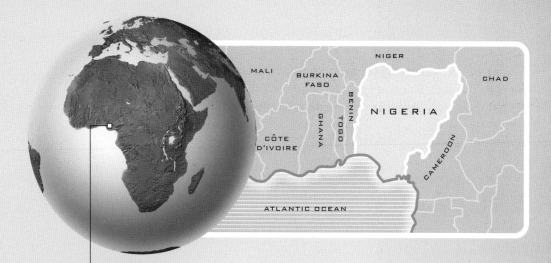

Nigeria

WHERE	Western Africa, bordering the Gulf of Guinea, between Benin and Cameroon
SIZE	923,768 sq km, slightly more than twice the size of California
POPULATION	137,253,133 *Note*: estimates for this country explicitly take into account the effects of excess mortality due to AIDS (July 2004 est.)
INFANT MORTALITY	70.49 deaths/1,000 live births
THE PEOPLE	Nigeria is composed of more than 250 ethnic groups; the following are the most populous and politically influential: Hausa and Fulani 29%, Yoruba 21%, Igbo (Ibo) 18%, Ijaw 10%, Kanuri 4%, Ibibio 3.5%, Tiv 2.5%
RELIGIONS	Muslim 50%, Christian 40%, indigenous beliefs 10%
LANGUAGES	English (official), Hausa, Yoruba, Igbo (Ibo), Fulani
LITERACY RATE	Total population: 68% male: 75.7% female: 60.6% (2003 est.)
GOVERNMENT	Republic transitioning from military to civilian rule
CAPITAL	Abuja

Abdul Wahab Matepo

Nigeria

42 years old, male, civil servant

Dear People of America,

I have often wondered about how lucky you people are. Aren't you lucky? You have a government that is ready to stand by its citizens, and you as a people are ready to break new ground in all fields of human endeavor to help mankind. You even shed blood for whoever you have decided to support. We Nigerians aren't that similar with you. In terms of those things regarded as "good" or "civilized," we are far behind. Whereas in those areas considered "bad" we are almost catching up with you. In fact, we have surpassed you in some areas.

There is corruption everywhere, agreed. But the level of corruption in Nigeria is much worse than in America. You must have heard about the millions of dollars we are trying to recover from our past leaders. It is very difficult for us to keep watch on our corruption because we have no free independent media like you do. In the American press, it was recently reported that President George W. Bush choked on a pretzel, fainted, and in the process got some bruises on his cheeks. No one would dare ascribe such a "misfortune" to a local government chairman in Nigeria, not to mention a state governor or his Excellency the President. Whoever reported such a thing would be lucky to lose only government patronage,

or have his premises burned down. In Nigeria, this news event will be proscribed. The president will be said to be on vacation. And on vacation he will be until his bruises have healed. You see, our countries are far apart in terms of openness. Neither do we always accept accidents or mishaps as natural. Perhaps Osama bin Laden should be held responsible for what happened to your president?

It is a pity that instead of copying such journalistic openness from your country, we have instead chosen to adopt your free and permissive culture. Hence, our ladies now go half-naked because it is also done in America. How much attention have you been paying to your family values? I learned that your rate of divorce and of single mothers is very high. The fabric of your social system and values is under threat. Why not learn from us how to uphold the institution of marriage and of family attachment? I have one wife. But I could have more, because in Nigeria polygamy is not a crime as it is in America. I have heard that there are 7.8 million more women than men in your country. It follows that if all your men were married, there are 7.8 million women who can't get a husband. Add to that your 20 million gay men and the fact that about 70% of your prison population is male. You can imagine the number of women who can't be married! Surely you need to find a solution to your problem of surplus women. President Clinton would not have been put through so much embarrassment over the Lewinsky affair if he was free to have more than one wife.

The fabric of your social system and values is under threat.

Do you Americans realize the good fortune you have with all your quality products? In Nigeria, we don't have such high standards. The road accident that I had in September 2000 would probably not have occurred if the bus I was traveling in was not fitted with expired, second-hand tires. Even if the accident had still occurred, as it does in your country too, I would have received immediate and adequate medical attention if I was in the U.S. Maybe I would not have been dumped in a government-owned tertiary hospital for twenty-four weeks, half of which was spent with nurses and trainees because the real doctors were on strike. I don't know if your medical professionals also abandon their patients and go on strike most of the time, like ours do. Even if they do, I'm sure that when they resume duties they will have access to the necessary equipment to attend to the needs of their patients.

As you can see, if we had your standards, many lives would not be wasted unnecessarily. And perhaps I would not have been paralyzed from my navel to my toes. And perhaps I would have been able to walk around. And perhaps I would not have the honor of being a member of the spinal cord injuries association of Nigeria. Surely we have a bit to learn from America.

But there is something that I don't understand about you

people. Why do you always want others to do things according to your wishes? During the regime of our General Babargida, you succeeded in bastardizing our currency, the Naria. You and your institutions, especially the IMF and the World Bank, said our Naria was over-valued. You pushed our leader until he devalued the Naria in 1986. Can you imagine what we have been suffering since the Naria was devalued via the so-called Structural Adjustment Programme (SAP)?

Don't you think it is better just to be grateful instead of grateful and arrogant?

I had just arrived in France when the SAP was introduced, and I was badly affected. I was expecting to spend one year there as part of my French language degree program at the University of Maiduguri in northern Nigeria. My relations and friends had pulled together all their resources to enable me to finance the program. But before my university authorities could transfer my money to France, the SAP was introduced. The result? The money that was meant for one year could no longer suffice. I had to return to Nigeria after only six weeks.

Have you ever recognized the fact that you are religious fanatics? Let me hasten to say that your religious fanaticism isn't the type we practice in Nigeria, where churches and mosques are burnt and many people are killed. But I strongly believe that you people have a bias for Christianity and the Jewish faith. Can't you remember how long it took the international community under your country's leadership to take decisive steps in the Bosnian crisis? You would not have waited that long if the victims were Jews or Christians, would you?

What of the humiliation being suffered every hour by the Palestinians? Isn't it because they are Muslims? I may not be very current, but I haven't heard of your president hosting Muslim children at the White House prior to the sad events of September 11, 2001. I'm sure you will never vote a Muslim into the White House in spite of your leadership position in the "democratic" world. I put it to you that these are the manifestations of your fanatical support for the church and the synagogue.

There is a saying in Yoruba language, probably borrowed from the Bible, which translates into something like, "arrogance precedes destruction." You people are too arrogant because of what God blessed you with. Don't you think it is better just to be grateful instead of grateful and arrogant? If you go through God's own books you will learn about the end of those who paraded themselves arrogantly before you.

You have contributed a lot to help mankind. Your legacies will help mankind and endure if you humble yourselves and treat all human beings as equal. Otherwise your fate won't be different from that of the other mighty nations of history.

Yours very truly,

Abdul Wahab Matepo

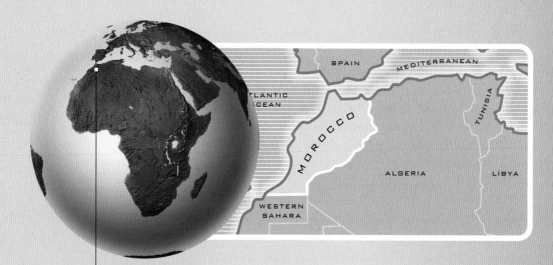

MOROCCO

WHERE	Northern Africa, bordering the North Atlantic Ocean and the Mediterranean Sea, between Algeria and Western Sahara
SIZE	446,550 sq km, slightly larger than California
POPULATION	32,209,101 (July 2004 est.)
INFANT MORTALITY	43.25 deaths/1,000 live births
THE PEOPLE	Arab-Berber 99.1%, other 0.7%, Jewish 0.2%
RELIGIONS	Muslim 98.7%, Christian 1.1%, Jewish 0.2%
LANGUAGES	Arabic (official), Berber dialects, French often the language of business, government, and diplomacy
LITERACY RATE	Total population: 52% (2003 est.)
GOVERNMENT	Constitutional monarchy
CAPITAL	Rabat

Mohamed Salem Soudani

Morocco

34 years old, male, Teacher

Dear People of America,

I was in your country two years ago and I was amazed at your hi-tech, your progress, and the various opportunities you have. I have seen how true and tangible the American dream was and continues to be.

Abundance is the very word in America. Any one of your Sunday papers has more pages than twenty national Moroccan papers put together. A city like Boston alone has more universities than my whole country. While you can have two or even three jobs at a time, dozens of young people from my country die and drown every year in their desperate trial to cross the Mediterranean. They prefer a decent death to a jobless life in our homeland. Still, no matter how hard the challenges my country faces, I am both lucky and proud to be Moroccan.

When I ask my students about what they want to do in the future, the answer so often is: go to America. I think I understand why. For them El Dorado is real and Paradise is no longer lost. If they could talk to you, they would tell you that you're lucky to be born in the country of boundless freedom, equal opportunities, and unparalleled justice.

Developed countries like yours should not take advantage of their economic supremacy to impose your culture, world view, and way of life on those less fortunate countries.

These were some of the things I marveled at when I traveled to your country. But after a few weeks there, the spell was broken. I found out that America is no place for me to work, nor a place to bring up my children. After all, there is nobody who would like to see their kids grow up not knowing their religion, forgetting their language, and ignoring their culture. I have seen many a Moroccan family in the States where children could no longer get along with their parents' beliefs and cultural values, refusing to speak Arabic, and at times hating even to be called Moroccan. I have the feeling that yours is a country that molds any diversity into a uniform whole, and where any divergence is illicitly condemned as downright un-American.

Moreover, many Americans come to settle in Morocco to get away from the hectic, too-worldly life in America. I had the chance to witness that for myself when I was there. In my relentless quest to do everything—work, study, travel—I realized that I forgot to do many more important things. In my religion and culture, I have a right on myself, my family has a right on me, and God has a right on me, too. In America, I couldn't give everybody their rights. I might have stuffed my mind with information, I could have overfed my body to obesity; but by doing so, I would have starved my soul to death.

I have the feeling that there is a great deal of hostility toward you in the world. At times, I am tempted to think it's due to envy. However, the more I ponder about it, the more I believe there are deeper reasons to it.

In your role as a unilateral leader of today's world, you have done a lot of good and a lot of bad. Moroccan soldiers have died side by side with GIs in World War II, and defeated Fascism and Nazism together with other free world allies. Yet, are the lives of Vietnamese, Somalians, and Iraqi kids cheaper than other lives? Would you accept any country to invade *your* land, capture *your* president, or change *your* political regime by force? I believe you explain many things with your economic interests, but it is a double-edged weapon if it is not guided by reason and responsibility. A leader should be strong, but he must be fair and just.

A leader should be strong, but he must be fair and just.

In this global village where we live, you are the unquestionable leader. The average citizen of our global village is awakened by an American clock, drives in an American automobile to go to work in an American multinational company. He watches Hollywood movies and listens to American music. He may be taking language courses at the American Language Center as he goes on wishing to find the American dream. It is unfortunate, however, to see that human cultural diversity is not given due care in our global village. I do not wish to see our *tanjia* and *couscous* give way only to Big Macs. I would still like to see our kids dance to the eternal rhythm of *gnawa* music.

I visited some of your high schools and was surprised that many of your students didn't know where my country was. They had no idea about our history, religion, philosophy, or culture. I believe that stereotypes and misconceptions arise when we don't know each other. Such is the case with Islam in the world today. I would like the whole world to understand the true image of Islamic religion and how it can be used to benefit humanity. Our new global system should be founded on values of mutual respect, appreciation, and balanced relationships. Developed countries like yours should not take advantage of their economic supremacy to impose your culture, world view, and way of life

I would like the whole world to understand the true image of Islamic religion and how it can be used to benefit humanity. Our new global system should be founded on values of mutual respect, appreciation, and balanced relationships.

Would you take a step forward and discover how different and, at the same time, how close we are?

on those less fortunate countries. Such injustice, rather than promote mutual understanding, will undoubtedly backfire in the long run.

We, at the other side of the Atlantic, hold your country and your culture in high respect and esteem. Would you take a step forward and discover how different and, at the same time, how close we are?

Very truly yours,

Mohamed Salem Soudani

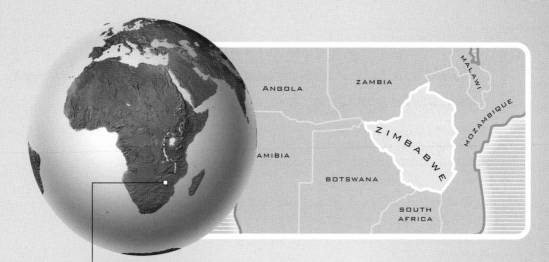

ZIMBABWE

WHERE	Southern Africa, between South Africa and Zambia
SIZE	390,580 sq km, slightly larger than Montana
POPULATION	12,671,860 *Note*: estimates for this country explicitly take into account the effects of excess mortality due to AIDS (July 2004 est.)
INFANT MORTALITY	67.08 deaths/1,000 live births
THE PEOPLE	African 98% (Shona 82%, Ndebele 14%, other 2%), mixed and Asian 1%, white less than 1%
RELIGIONS	Syncretic (part Christian, part indigenous beliefs) 50%, Christian 25%, indigenous beliefs 24%, Muslim and other 1%
LANGUAGES	English (official), Shona, Sindebele (the language of the Ndebele), numerous but minor tribal dialects
LITERACY RATE	Total population: 90.7% male: 94.2% female: 87.2% (2003 est.)
GOVERNMENT	Parliamentary democracy
CAPITAL	Harare

TENDAI MUCHIN

ZIMBABWE

20 YEARS OLD, MALE, COLLEGE STUDENT

Dear People of America,

I am glad to write this letter to you. I have got a lot to say to you at this juncture when there is so much happening in Zimbabwe and the world. As I write this, it seems as if I have suddenly realized how your country never ceases to amaze me. Such a vast melting pot, highly developed and yet humble and realistic in its outlook of itself and others. You will not come to fully appreciate the power of American influence on thinking and actions in the developing world until you are introduced to this, my troubled homeland, small and landlocked as it is near the southernmost tip of Africa.

Here in Zimbabwe, the United States of America is the ultimate dream land. A land of many opportunities where fame and fortune are made. Although it goes some way further, the Americanization of the Zimbabwean society has taken its heaviest toll on the young generation of the upper classes. That group of people, some of them really look straight out of the streets of New York. Let me not beat about the bush here, the Americanization is in the fancy dressing and lifestyle, baggy pants and multi-coloured shirts for the guys, and for the chicks, tights and chains. Those brands are really expensive, but I wouldn't dress like that if I had the money; I'm kind of conservative.

All that violence, drugs, and extravagance portrayed in your music videos and lyrics have won hearts, and people try to imitate it.

American influence on this group of people has reached high levels. They know every detail about American hip hop and idealize its stars whom they have made roll models. They dream of the day they'll meet R Kelly or work for Russell Simmons. They are sometimes referred to as "nosies," because when they speak it appears to be coming out assisted by the nose, sounding more like the accent of white people or first language English speakers. And the slang—you just cannot keep up pace with it. Some of them I really wonder if they can speak a full sentence of our local language.

What is most saddening is that what is portrayed on the American films shown on satellite television (that is subscription television) is not real life and is exaggerated. All that violence, drugs, and extravagance portrayed in your music videos and lyrics have won hearts, and people try to imitate it.

I go to a popular college in the capital city, Harare. One day like I always do I went early to use the library and I witnessed an incident that reminded me of a scene from *Higher Learning*, a movie starring my favorite actor, Laurence Fishburne.

A fight broke out between two groups of high school students, drawing a helpless crowd of students and members of staff. They were running uncontrollably at each other in and outside of buildings, shouting abuses at each other in obscene language. I'm saying in the States those are real emotions; I mean with those racial attacks, killings, and all the traumatizing incidents that you can come to expect in such a vast and diverse country. These students at my college had never been exposed to a life of violence, drugs, and casual sex. It has been thrown into their faces on the telly, where they've been shown how it's done in the American colleges and ghettos. They don't even know how it is like in *our own* ghettos.

I almost forgot about something that I wanted to tell you. There is this issue about salads in Zimbabwe. Salads. Salad is a name given to young people from well-to-do families and yuppies. The name is an abbreviation of "Stupid African Learning American Doings." Most of them are offended, of course, but some take it as envious acknowledgement of their privileges. People perceived to be salads have been a target of unruly attacks—from being stripped naked of their mini-skirts to being verbally abused. Salad is a household word in Zimbabwe. But these days, a little luxury can earn you the salad tag. Some of my less pleasant friends like calling me that in relation to my passion for the game cricket, once reserved for whites.

I think that the changing scenes in your country is as a result of your strong desire to learn new things and the determination to improve your lives. The desire to improve our situation is evident in my countrymen, too, and we will help ourselves by following the American example.

Zimbabwe is similar to America in its society composition, which is somewhat multi-racial. The population is predominantly black, but there is a small but vibrant white population of British and Dutch ancestry. Obviously, race is a big issue. I like the way that Americans use their good humor to discuss the racial issue, which I think makes people see things in a lighter manner and helps to ease racial tension and suspicions. I enjoy

… the changing scenes in your country is as a result of your strong desire to learn new things and the determination to improve your lives.

how the thirty-year–old white senior pastor at our multi-racial church likes to make jokes and gets away with it just like those hilarious characters from American sitcoms. He is able to make both blacks and whites laugh at themselves.

There is great misrule, violence, and corruption happening in Zimbabwe. Our presidential elections are widely regarded as having been flawed in favor of the sitting president and eventual winner Robert Mugabe. But in all fairness, if there were any irregularities at all in the American elections, they cannot be compared to ours. Prior to the actual voting, there was widespread violence and intimidation of opposition supporters that resulted in some loss of life. Toward the election days, some of the main opposition party candidate supporters organized a peaceful march in the streets of central Harare. But a group of marauding ruling party supporters besieged the city centre to stop the march. A confrontation started, sending people running all over the place. I happened to be in town that day and I wasn't so lucky. I was struck by a tree-branch stick across my back, giving me a swollen and very painful arm.

For the first time, I was eligible to vote, and believe it or not, some of us had to wait for sixteen hours to cast our votes.

For the first time, I was eligible to vote, and believe it or not, some of us had to wait for sixteen hours to cast our votes. In what was believed to be an act to discourage urban voters, the opposition's stronghold, there were less than half the polling stations in each constituency from the last parliamentary elections. The queues were very long and a good number were not very patient. My friend and I went to the polling station at around one p.m. on Saturday, but our chance came at five a.m. on Sunday. One can only wonder what would have happened in response to these things in a democracy such as yours. Some pro-government intellectuals have said that Western and American type of liberties do not apply to us, but I say no, democracy is democracy and human rights are the same everywhere. These are universal concerns.

But in all these I think that what Americans, or anybody for that matter, can learn from Zimbabweans is their endurance in the face of trouble and hardships. People have patiently waited for peaceful and swift transformation that will not cause further damage and bloodshed. Any act of force will result in total collapse.

Hey, let me just comment on the Iraqi war before I go. A lot has been said about it here, but no one has really come out objectively on the whole issue. I'm talking about the local commentators; their views had been biased. For them, it has been a case of which side are you on, really? Are you anti-American? Are you anti-Moslem? In fact, in a nationwide survey conducted by a pressure group led by a pro-government man, it came out that 98% of the Zimbabwe population are against the war's devastating nature and deaths of civilians. But out of that, 68% believe the busting of Saddam Hussein's regime is justifiable. I wonder how you, regular citizens, really feel about these acts. I don't think the TV can give me a fair understanding of your feelings. I hope this letter gave you some ideas about mine.

Your friend,

Tendai Muchin

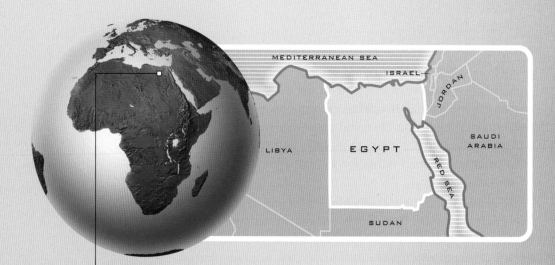

EGYPT

Mohamed Shaheen

Egypt

35 years old, male, e-commerce specialist

Dear People of America,

I am a Muslim and thirty-five years old. I have lived in many different countries; I have lived in the U.S.A. I enjoy reading. I especially like civilization and business books.

After spending time in your country, I think it is a wonderful idea for people in the world to write to you and let you hear our voices. I think in spite of the U.S.A. being the most powerful country in the world, American people live in their islands and don't know what's happening in the world. It was surprising to you to see the collapsing of the World Trade Center, and you started to ask, "Why do others hate us? What's going on?"

It is important to be interested in other parts of our world. I have many questions that I think are important to consider. When the U.S.A. attacked Iraq, they didn't find any dangerous weapons. So, why did the U.S.A. do that? Why did the American media make Saddam Hussain an enemy? I think many people in the world are asking these questions—are you?

The problem that comes up between our cultures is Israel. The U.S.A. has supported Israel for a long time against Muslims. Israel has played the game very well, because they succeeded in controlling the opinions of the

I think in spite of the U.S.A. being the most powerful country in the world, American people live in their islands and don't know what's happening in the world.

American people through the media, Congress, and many other organizations. It's hard not to believe that the U.S.A. follows Israel's interests, because they have interests of their own. Have you asked yourselves, "What are the interests of the American government, are they my interests? Is this good for the rest of the world, not just the U.S.A.?"

I am grateful that I've learned so much from U.S.A. technology. I work as an e-commerce specialist. Your country is a great supporter of science and technology. You gave us a lot in this field. But, I think you need the morals, the values of Islam. You need Islam values as we need your science and technology. I've met three Americans in Egypt. After the 11 September event, they came to Egypt to know Islam better, they embraced Islam, and they said to me, "You have a great religion. We need this religion badly in the U.S.A." Islam is not only a religion, it is a way of life.

Your laws that collect all your states together is the strength in your country. I think the people who created it are great people. They loved your country and were creative too. I like the freedom of American people. You can say what you want, do what you like any time you like—this is great. If this freedom was governed by good morals, it would give your community better results. From my point of view, the weakest part of your community is that dollars are the most powerful effective value there, more important than the relation between man and woman. The ties between families are not warm enough, and family rule is going to disappear. I think you need the women to rule in her house, where she can provide more for her children and husband. I think women in your country need the warmth of the family, of the house, warmth of her husband and children. Everybody there runs towards dollars, and life without settlement and the warmth of family is hard.

I am not proficient in English writing so I can't express well everything that I want to say. People in my community like Americans because they gave us a lot. Unfortunately, I think you have started to lose this love and respect because of your government policy, which doesn't respect other people.

Thank you for listening,

Mohamed

Niger

WHERE	Western Africa, southeast of Algeria
SIZE	1.267 million sq km, slightly less than twice the size of Texas
POPULATION	11,360,538 (July 2004 est.)
INFANT MORTALITY	122.66 deaths/1,000 live births
THE PEOPLE	Religions Muslim 80%, remainder indigenous beliefs and Christian
RELIGIONS	Hausa 56%, Djerma 22%, Fula 8.5%, Tuareg 8%, Beri Beri (Kanouri) 4.3%, Arab, Toubou, and Gourmantche 1.2%, about 1,200 French expatriates
LANGUAGES	Languages: French (official), Hausa, Djerma
LITERACY RATE	Total population: 17.6% male: 25.8% female: 9.7% (2003 est.)
GOVERNMENT	Republic
CAPITAL	Niamey

Adem

Niger

Age: When asked his age, he answered, "It is more important how wise you are then how long you have been living on the earth." The Targi do not count their age. His interpreters guessed that he may be close to twenty-eight years old. male, nomadic Targi

(Dear people of America)

↓

(Adem, tribe Kel Tedeli)

Dear people of America,

I wish to thank you, the people of America, because you support peace. The leaders of your country deserve no thanks. Sometimes when Americans visit my country, the Sahara, they talk a lot and they bring a lot of stuff. We Tuareg live simply and by our virtues. America doesn't have virtues they live by. That's why the people are lost. Sometimes they are afraid to sleep out under the stars; they aren't friends with nature anymore. We can learn a lot from them and they can learn a lot from us.

I have seen pictures of the Natives in your country. They are similar to us. They are beautiful, they are our brothers. One day we will reunite with them. All the people with pure hearts are our brothers.

Adem

I wish to thank you, the people of America, because you support peace.

Sometimes they are afraid to sleep out under the stars;
they aren't friends with nature anymore.

CAMEROON

WHERE	Western Africa, bordering the Bight of Biafra, between Equatorial Guinea and Nigeria
SIZE	475,440 sq km, slightly larger than California
POPULATION	16,063,678 *Note*: estimates for this country explicitly take into account the effects of excess mortality due to AIDS (July 2004 est.)
INFANT MORTALITY	69.18 deaths/1,000 live births
THE PEOPLE	Cameroon Highlanders 31%, Equatorial Bantu 19%, Kirdi 11%, Fulani 10%, Northwestern Bantu 8%, Eastern Nigritic 7%, other African 13%, non-African less than 1%
RELIGIONS	Indigenous beliefs 40%, Christian 40%, Muslim 20%
LANGUAGES	24 major language groups, English and French (official)
LITERACY RATE	Total population: 79% male: 84.7% female: 73.4% (2003 est.)
GOVERNMENT	Unitary republic; multiparty presidential regime
CAPITAL	Yaounde

JEAN MARIE TETIO

CAMEROON

21 YEARS OLD, MALE, COLLEGE STUDENT

Dear People of America,

I am much delighted with this opportunity given me to address you. In fact, to me America is like the father of all countries and I see it to be a dream land, a place where many people around the world have hopes of living one day. There are so many aspects which have made many people around the world willing to die because of the love they have for America, while others on their part have lived to hate America. My discussion therefore attempts a look at the merits and demerits about your country and how I feel about it.

Your culture has done a great deal to many countries of the world. For example, in Africa the way of life of the people has been drastically changed because of American influence. This change has several dimensions—like dressing, way of talking, dancing, etc. I can also remember how my grandfather told me how they used to dress with bark of trees but today they wear good dresses. All this has come about thanks to the invention of telecommunication gadgets like the television which opened another window of the world. African American movies and other TV programs have greatly taught us a lot about your culture. This was done by simply comparing the way we see you people do things with ours and wherever we found ourselves wanting we made the necessary adjustments. Today

Now that you know how to respect your people's privacy so well, why must you come into other people's matters too?

my social life has changed. I now go to night clubs with snacks, dancing, drinking alcoholic beer, and having sex with different girls. Things have never been like this before. I could never have a relationship with a girl if I was not married, nor drink alcohol.

Your religion too has brought about a great change in my country and the rest of Africa in general. Yesteryears idolatry used to be the main feature in African traditional religion, and this practice used to lead at times to a lot of human rights abuses, like the sacrificing of twins and female genital mutilation. However, with the introduction of your Western Christianity here, all these practices have long ceased to exist, and people have taken on the worship of a Supreme Being. Today I have taken on Christian beliefs. I can remember a story my great grandfather told me concerning their formal religion. He said, at the end of every nine months of a year a sacrifice was made to their god, Ushim. A young virgin girl of age at least fifteen was caught and offered to their god. There was a messenger from the god that will deliver a message to the king who he wants for the sacrifice and the king will immediately send his guards to arrest the person. After the arrest, the messenger announces to the people who is to be offered that year. If the sacrifice is not made in time, the god, Ushim, becomes very angry and people start starving and dying randomly.

Another thing which is really a marvel here is your technology and amazing knowledge of how things work. This is illustrated in the various forms of new communication technology you have brought here. There is the Internet, mobile communication, satellite, etc. This has really made the world a global village and I think if not, the idea of *Letters to America* would never have reached me.

America is a womb which has brought forth people of great character who can and have changed the phases of history by bringing development and changes to other nations of the world. Your role in the abolition of the apartheid regime in South Africa and the release of Mandela from prison is a glaring example. The quest for global peace inherent in your policies is really a blessing to the world. This can be seen in your mediation of several conflict resolutions. My friends and family find the U.S. policy very good, interesting, and encouraging. The fight for democracy and dictatorship in other countries helps to reduce poverty, thus enabling a growth of the country's economy. Also, I do hear people talk about the U.S. government. Some are encouraging the government while some are criticizing. I remember when I was listening to a conversation

> *America is a womb which has brought forth people of great character who can and have changed the phases of history by bringing development and changes to other nations of the world.*

between two French journalists over a French radio station. They were criticizing the U.S. government of focusing their mind on benefits from other countries, taking an example with Iraq, saying that the U.S. aim was to benefit from their oil and not to disarm the country. For me in particular, I find that your system of government is the best, and I wish that God always blesses you for your enormous efforts towards other countries.

Furthermore, your education system is to the world like nectar is to bees. No wonder many people are scrambling to come and study in America. I had a friend with whom I used to study in secondary school. This guy was so shy and in fact so fragile that we nicknamed him "mummy's son." After secondary school he went to America for further studies, and when he came back to Cameroon he was a changed man. He had grown more mature, he was so bold, and most importantly he had a sense of independence. He became the admiration of everybody around him.

Now from what I have just said it seems like America is a land where there is no cause for sorrow. Far from this, because there are people who would be willing to die because of their hatred for America. Experience has shown that life in America can really be dangerously insecure. Today one can find not less than 5,000 students in America who are in possession of guns and firearms. The general idea is that if you have a misunderstanding with somebody what happens is that he just blows off your head with a gun. I once read a story about how a fifteen-year-old boy killed an old man of fifty-seven. When taken to court, the young man gave what sounds like nonsense to me as reason for killing the old man. "He just got angry when he saw anyone with a beard." This is what makes most people hate America. It makes people afraid to come to America. America, you are really too contradictory at times.

From what I know about life there, many people never like people poking their noses into their affairs because they want their privacy. This is reflected in societal daily interactions. A man's problems are his alone and no one has the right to come asking questions without being invited to do so. Now that you know how to respect your people's privacy so well, *America, you are really too contradictory at times.* why must you come into other people's matters too? When it comes to conflicts in other countries you are the first to rush here as if you are the world's police. It is not really bad when you are trying to mediate for the sake of peace, but must you take sides? See what happened between Iraq and Kuwait; was it worth that to make you Iraq's enemy? At times you also go the lengths of inspecting the arms of other nations as if you can also allow them to inspect yours, too. This is not fair. The fact that you have a military might does not make you a player and a referee at the same time. Things like this give you a very bad face in the world's eyes, thus instigating bitterness in peoples' minds about your country.

But still, America remains the dream land, where every soul would like to one day breathe the cool fresh and inspiring air along the Mississippi or stroll in front of the Liberty Statue! Wow, America the dream and … land of my dreams.

Jean Marie Tetio

Mali

WHERE	Western Africa, southwest of Algeria
SIZE	1.24 million sq km, slightly less than twice the size of Texas
POPULATION	11,956,788 (July 2004 est.)
INFANT MORTALITY	117.99 deaths/1,000 live births
THE PEOPLE	Mande 50% (Bambara, Malinke, Soninke), Peul 17%, Voltaic 12%, Songhai 6%, Tuareg and Moor 10%, other 5%
RELIGIONS	Muslim 90%, indigenous beliefs 9%, Christian 1%
LANGUAGES	French (official), Bambara 80%, numerous African languages
LITERACY RATE	Total population: 46.4% male: 53.5% female: 39.6% (2003 est.)
GOVERNMENT	Republic
CAPITAL	Bamako

JOB AMAGOIN TESSOUGUE

MALI

40 YEARS OLD, MALE, MALARIA RESEARCH
CENTER MANAGER

Dear People of America,

It is with a very great honor that I am writing to you. I am a manager in a center which is doing research against malaria in Bamako, the capital city of Mali. I have the opportunity to meet many Americans for the simple reason that I am managing a guesthouse for students and researchers linked to this project.

Many Malians, as I am, are thinking that America is a great nation, a symbol of economic power. It's a country where one can get a lot of dollars when you work hard. It's thought to be a country where a Malian cannot enter because it is heavily locked to strangers.

The economic power of the U.S.A. gives certain sufficiency and a complex of superiority. It is often obvious that many Americans have truncated views about Africa and poor countries like Mali. Americans think that Africa is a continent of wars, hunger, bad living conditions. When they come in Mali, some Americans refuse to eat our meals or don't want to make a friend. Once a young American came here and she refused to enter the toilets that all her comrades used when they went to visit the villages. When she came back in Bamako she rushed into the camping toilet. During her stay there she ate only biscuits.

Malian newspapers do not comment on bad aspects of Americans' politics. But in general people think that America is a proud nation. When Americans get in trouble with another nation, people think that it is a religious problem. September 11 is considered as Islam's victory over Christians.

Americans are surprised to see a Malian speak English, French, and two other regional languages, but this is what they find. Americans are amazed to see a Malian intellectual who speaks two or three languages, because in America they speak one and only one language. Our educational system permits our students to learn many languages at the same time!

Life in Mali is quite different from American life. In Mali, we give priority to the social aspect that is large family. We eat in the same plate and wash our hands together.

There is an aspect of our society that amazes young Americans during their stay in Mali: that is the fact that people joke with one another. Joking cousin relationships play a very important role in interpersonal relations. There are joking cousin relationships between ethnic groups, between families, and among members of family. Joking serves to diffuse any tension that can be present in a social situation. For example, the Bozo (ethnic group) are joking cousins of the Dogons (ethnic group) in Mali. To joke here means telling something to make other people laugh, but the fact is deeper than a simple laugh. It means to tease each other verbally and physically. The joking cousins can even insult each other, but never quarrel. They have absolute tolerance for each other. Joking cousins are considered to be not able to harm each other because of the innate tolerance they have for each other. So, the meaning of joking cousins is very deep. It is because of this relation they are successful mediators between them. After the intervention of a Bozo in an inter-Dogon conflict, the Dogon must make peace. When I say to make peace that means to stop the dispute. It's the same for the Bozo to accept a Dogon-signed peace. A Dogon can be a mediator between two Bozos in conflict and a Bozo can also do the same thing. The Diarra and the Traore families are joking cousins, as are the Touré and Kéita.

Americans should open themselves to other cultures. The discovery of neighbors and other cultures is a positive factor of happiness and open mindedness. You must create partnerships and friendship with other African countries. Today it is very difficult for a Malian to go to America. A visa is not easy—or impossible—to get. One of my cousins has been attempting to go there for two years, but no way. He is registered in two universities there, but Americans do not let him go. They hardened the door of their visa to discourage every person who longs to go there. Is America really Eldorado?

My family has the same vision of America as me. Our living style is too different from Americans. It is quite impossible to live here without greeting or helping one another. Here you cannot pass near someone without giving a salutation. My parents agree that working in America is possible but forbid that any of us should forget one's culture. Personally, I find it difficult to adopt American culture where everybody minds his own business, and his brother is ignored.

I find it difficult to adopt American culture where everybody minds his own business, and his brother is ignored.

Friendly,

Job Amagoin Tessougue

ASIA

INDIA

PAKISTAN

BANGLADESH

AZERBAIJAN

UZBEKISTAN

JAPAN

CHINA

SOUTH
KOREA

TAIWAN

M. Brecke

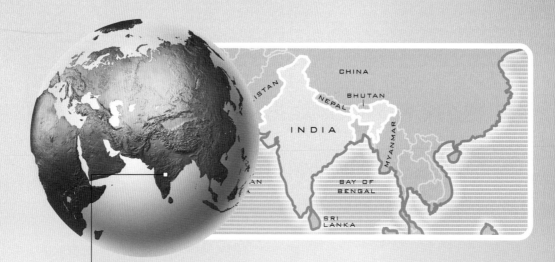

INDIA

WHERE	Southern Asia, bordering the Arabian Sea and the Bay of Bengal, between Burma and Pakistan
SIZE	3,287,590 sq km, slightly more than one-third the size of the U.S.
POPULATION	1,065,070,607 (July 2004 est.)
INFANT MORTALITY	57.92 deaths/1,000 live births
THE PEOPLE	Indo-Aryan 72%, Dravidian 25%, Mongoloid and other 3%
RELIGIONS	Hindu 81.3%, Muslim 12%, Christian 2.3%, Sikh 1.9%, other groups including Buddhist, Jain, Parsi 2.5%
LANGUAGES	English enjoys associate status but is the most important language for political and commercial communication; Hindi is the national language and primary tongue of 30% of the people; there are fourteen other official languages
LITERACY RATE	Total population: 59.5% male: 70.2% female: 48.3% (2003 est.)
GOVERNMENT	Federal republic
CAPITAL	New Delhi

Mitra Muralidhran

India

34 years old, female, freelance journalist
for The Times of India

Dear People of America,

When you think of India you may think of a country that is poor in comparison to yours. But I am proud to say that I am an Indian born in a culturally rich and diverse India. This richness is like a tapestry inlaid with ancient languages, innumerable communities, traditions and lifestyles. Our diversity is our beauty and despite our differences, we are all imbibed with a strong cultural value. I watch myself and my culture change due to Western life influences, but still most of us respect elders, live in a joint family system, and are very hospitable in nature.

But for me, dear Americans, you too seem to be rich. I am not talking from the economic point of view. From my country comes a nurturing of the spirit, from yours a cultivation of the mind. I love your broad-minded attitude toward other countries and their people. Terrorists took advantage of that nature and had the guts to strike you. After that you realized how terrorist activities really affect people physically and economically. Terrorism in our Kashmir has been going on for the last two decades and many a time, when we sought your intervention in this matter, you turned a blind eye and deaf ears. Your government was like a child pretending to be asleep. But when the same problem happened to you, you woke up from your slumber. I would like to say to you, "good morning."

One element in you, dear Americans, which is very nice, is your unity in times of calamity. Your genuine interest in helping others is really admirable. Sadly, when it comes to relationships with your own family members, especially marital relationships, you develop lion-sized egos and spoil it first, then brood over it. Think of us. We just ignore many things in our life. Ignorance is really bliss. When one fights the other keeps quiet. It's a very small adjustment! Another thing is about empathy. When your spouse fights have empathy for her/him. If you practice this technique, you'll see your divorce rate dropping. I want to tell you about our wonderful joint family system which is being followed even today in many parts of our country. This system binds family members, teaches love, selflessness, and so much more. Good families make for a good society.

Since America is the most powerful nation in the world, its future will severely affect other nations.

Have you heard the story about the Samantha family? They have a strong force of over 140 family members respectively living under one roof. Living this way, people learn valuable lessons in flexibility, efficient administration, managerial skills, belongingness and familial love. Every day over a hundred people from the age group of ninety years to two months gather in the large dinner room that occupies the entire ground floor of that building in batches, since it cannot accommodate them all at one time. You'll be amazed to know that the entire family uses 50 kgs of vegetables, 20 kgs of wheat flour, 25 kgs of rice, 25 litres of milk—comprising one meal of a day. Recognized by the Calcutta Municipal Corporation as the single largest family, the Samanthas live in the heart of Calcutta eating out of a single kitchen. The 140 member family chalk out their responsibilities and do wonderful work. For example, there are heads for each and every area like education, finance, food and entertainment, management of children, etc. And, they make sure that the thread of oneness is running through them perennially.

Like the Samanthas, there are many joint families existing in India. These family structures stand as an example of selfless love. So, our dear people of America, if you want to improve the value of family system, don't you think you should remain united? I know Americans, like the people of all developed countries, are highly independent by nature. Most of your families have both the parents working and in that case, perhaps you are putting material things above the bond of man and woman. This leads to fighting. Whom do you think it'll affect? Of course, your children. There are many ways that you bring up children that are also admirable. Truly, I am awed by the way many of you single-handedly bring up your children even after being separated from your spouse. But if you want to have happy family lives try to go for a joint family system. Then there is always support for everyone. I'll not say in India everything is fantastic. The 30-percent urban populace is seeing more divorces now, thanks to the Western culture. Western culture encourages

us to have nuclear families, and makes us long for riches. Longing for material wealth eventually leads us to have less time for the family and more tiffs and ultimately, a surge in the divorce rates. So, all Indians don't have any right to advise you.

Earlier, I told you how I admire your way of bringing up the children. Agreed that we Indians have strong family values, but in India, bringing up a child is casually done—where as in America you give a lot of weight to their overall development.

As far as spirituality is concerned, no doubt we are rich. Late George Harrison knew it very well and you Americans know it, too. It's obvious by the presence of so many spiritual centers in your country offering discourses on techniques like yoga. I am very happy you are willing to take the essence of India's spirituality and practice it in your life. It's possible only because of your broad mindedness and interest to learn. Dear friends, practicing "Ahimsa" and "Yoga" will do a lot of good for you. "Ahimsa" is the concept of not killing or harming any living thing. In times of calamity, practicing Ahimsa will give you a lot of strength. Says our spiritual guru, Swami Sivananda, trial and difficulties are bound to come in your way to test your strength. You should stand adamant. Then alone will your efforts be crowned with sanguine success. There is a hidden power in Ahimsa which protects its practitioners. The invisible hand of God gives protection. There is no fear. What can pistols and swords do? I feel he'd say this to you. It's heartening to hear that more and more Americans are turning vegetarian and following Ahimsa, and our younger generation who are always in awe of you have started realizing the goodness of our spirituality and its mightiness. Thanks to the people of America! You have helped us to understand our own spirituality and this encourages us to explore the subject in depth.

But a sad fact is that back in your country, multinational companies vie with each other to employ Indian nationals because, in spite of higher academic qualifications and smart brains, the pay package is cheaper than employing whites. Color of the skin rules the roost. Racism is very much there, even if you want to believe that it's not. Just ask any black or Indian person in America and it is clearly true. My advice is that you please see the mind and soul of a person, not the color of their skin!

My advice is that you please see the mind and soul of a person, not the color of their skin!

Given a chance I would love to visit this warm, friendly, hospitable and lovely America to know her better in every way. To conclude, dear people of America, when I think of you, I remember what Winston Churchill once said, "Courage is what it takes to stand up and speak. Courage is also what it takes to sit down and listen."

Thanks so much for listening!

Mitra

PAKISTAN

WHERE	Southern Asia, bordering the Arabian Sea, between India on the east and Iran and Afghanistan on the west and China in the north
SIZE	803,940 sq km, slightly less than twice the size of California
POPULATION	159,196,336 (July 2004 est.)
INFANT MORTALITY	74.43 deaths/1,000 live births
THE PEOPLE	Punjabi, Sindhi, Pashtun (Pathan), Baloch, Muhajir (immigrants from India at the time of partition and their descendants)
RELIGIONS	Muslim 97% (Sunni 77%, Shi'a 20%), Christian, Hindu, other 3%
LANGUAGES	Punjabi 48%, Sindhi 12%, Siraiki (a Punjabi variant) 10%, Pashtu 8%, Urdu (official) 8%, Balochi 3%, Hindko 2%, Brahui 1%, English (official and lingua franca of Pakistani elite and most government ministries), Burushaski, other 8%
LITERACY RATE	Total population: 45.7% male: 59.8% female: 30.6% (2003 est.)
GOVERNMENT	Federal republic
CAPITAL	Islamabad

KHALID

PAKISTAN

21 YEARS OLD, MALE, PREMEDICAL STUDENT

Dear People of America, ·

I have a friend, Mike, who lives in New York; he always used to come to Peshawar, Pakistan. He has a huge antique shop in New York, which is why he travels to the Asian countries to buy antiques. Whenever I met Mike, we discussed different matters, but he always avoided talking about politics.

One day, I don't remember the exact date, but it was after the American strikes on Iraq, we were sitting in my shop. We were very busy counting silver rings and necklaces. Suddenly, Mike put the silver rings to one side and asked me a question that made me laugh but also confused. Mike asked me what I think about him. I laughed and said that I think that he is a human being. He ran his fingers through his hair and said that there is no doubt that he is a human being and no one says that he is a monkey! From Mike's reaction I come to know that he expects more words.

He asked me with a more serious expression, what is my feeling for him, his country and government. I shook my head and started to explain about my view. I told Mike, what I think about him is that he is a human being and all human beings deserve their rights, regardless of their gender, religion and nationality; about his country, I think that I should respect every country and same with your country. Regarding the government, I give him more explanation that encouraged Mike to ask me more questions. I told him that when America, I mean U.S.A., attacked Afghanistan, I was thinking that government of America is a democracy-loving state and wants to help every nation to enjoy it as they are. When U.S.A. started to attack Iraq, my previous opinion was totally changed and I came to know I was stupid to be tricked by their speeches and never think about the real base of a matter. Also I come to know that U.S. government is like a beast that steps on everything to get oil and enlarge her empire.

Americans ... only depend on their own media and think that every place on the earth is same like their country. This is true especially with the teenage group that is making the future of the tomorrow.

Mike went on and asked me what I dislike and like about his country. I started laughing and asked him why he is asking me these questions, is he thinking that besides selling antiques he should start another job of being a journalist to gain more money? He replied to me that he wants to have a clear mentality and improve himself. So I told him that what I like about Americans is that they never interfere in your personal life. And what I dislike about them is that they severely ignore the rest of the world. They only depend on their own media and think that every place on the earth is same like their country. This is true especially with the teenage group that is making the future of the tomorrow.

Mike looked at his watch and told me that he has to meet a friend, but before leaving he wants to ask a last question. He asked what advice I can give to him and other Americans. I paused for a moment and then told him that you should learn from our big mistake. Never to interfere religion with state and try to have a secular state. You, the people, are the ones that can put pressure on your government to stop invading the world for the sake of oil. This profit of oil will be never shared with you and all of it will go to the pocket of multi-national companies and the government.

You, the people, are the ones that can put pressure on your government to stop invading the world for the sake of oil.

I was happy to answer his questions for Mike and I am happy to share these thoughts with all of you.

Khalid

BANGLADESH

WHERE	Southern Asia, bordering the Bay of Bengal, between Myanmar and India
SIZE	144,000 sq km, slightly smaller than Iowa
POPULATION	141,340,476 (July 2004 est.)
INFANT MORTALITY	64.32 deaths/1,000 live births
THE PEOPLE	Bengali 98%, tribal groups, non-Bengali Muslims
RELIGIONS	Muslim 83%, Hindu 16%, other 1%
LANGUAGES	Bangla (official, also known as Bengali), English
LITERACY RATE	Total population: 43.1% male: 53.9% female: 31.8% (2003 est.)
GOVERNMENT	Parliamentary democracy
CAPITAL	Dhaka

Selina Hossain

Bangladesh

56 years old, female, writer, director of the Bangla Academy in Dhaka

Dear People of America,

When the plane landed in San Francisco, it was very late. My daughter and her husband were eagerly waiting at the arrival gate to greet me. Their first child was due any day, and I had made the long journey in order to be with them for the delivery. The baby's father is a Canadian while my daughter is Bangladeshi. The baby is going to be an American by birth. I am delighted to find such a unity of nations within one family—two countries living under one roof as a family with a third country soon to be added.

When we left the airport, there was a mild chill in the air, which felt strangely thin compared to the heavy air of my native Dhaka. As we headed for their home in the city, the car traveled over a beautiful road that twisted around the hills. A thousand shimmering lights lit the dark of a sleeping city. My tired eyes struggled to absorb every detail of the landscape through which we passed. As I stepped into their home, I felt there was something welcoming in the whole environment, which wrapped around me like a warm shawl. I instantly felt part of this extraordinary city and its people. This very feeling was confirmed with various experiences that I am going to describe in the following sections.

I have known Americans as people of kind hearts, with a remarkable love for children, a deep respect for the independence of other nations, and a readiness to assist those who are forced into a war.

My daughter made regular visits to the University of California San Francisco Medical Center for her prenatal check-ups. Days passed, and my daughter passed her due date with no sign of delivery. We passed the days by keeping as busy as we could. We visited the campus of the University of California Berkeley, as well as a popular baby store to buy last-minute items for the newborn. I was amazed by the choice of products—things never imagined in Bangladesh.

One evening, my daughter went to the hospital when the baby, which until then had been very active in her stomach, seemed to stop moving. I rushed to the hospital to find my daughter in the recovery room and the baby in intensive care, delivered by emergency surgery and placed on a respirator. The baby was being attended by some of the best doctors in the United States, his condition precarious. Despite everything the doctors said about the baby's condition, I could not believe that anything was wrong when his sparkling dark eyes met mine.

What struck me most was their determination to save the lives of the babies. I had often heard and believed the saying that love, devotion, and care cannot be bought at any price, yet here were medical specialists providing all these gifts in their professional capacity. Their devotion went well beyond what they are paid to do. I admired their sense of duty for the well-being of the babies in the ICU, the patience with which they endured the physical and other demands places on them, their timeliness, and even the occasional touches of superstition that infused their work. Whereas in Bangladesh many newborns die every day, among them some are simply because of sheer negligence on medical doctors' part.

I was fortunate indeed to know these wonderful American health care providers, each of whom were very special in their own way. One nurse would regularly call the teenaged mother of a six-month old baby who had a major heart operation, urging her to visit more regularly. Once I heard her insist: "You are a mother. I can do everything except give your daughter the joy of a mother's touch." Another nurse brought my daughter a Polaroid photograph of the baby, as an effective psychological boost to help her pump her first mother's milk.

I was equally fortunate to meet other wonderful Americans on my previous visits to your country. I remember the New York taxi driver who contributed to Bangladesh's struggle for liberation by attending the Concert for Bangladesh organized by George Harrison at Madison Square Garden. I was touched to know he played his own small part in the process that made us an independent nation and that he remembered the events of a war fought on the other side of the world.

I have known Americans as people of kind hearts, with a remarkable love for children, a deep respect for the independence of other nations, and a readiness to assist those who are forced into a war. With the approach of the Iraq war, I wondered how a country's leaders could press for war with another country. How could they knowing how many children will be killed? This seemed in contradiction to the kindness of the American people that I had known and admired. I am happy to find that Americans who believe in the primacy of peace, over any other means to bring justice to the world, raised their voices in protest. I only wish that the voices of those conscientious people were heard and heeded.

Selina Hossain

Azerbaijan

WHERE	Southwestern Asia, bordering the Caspian Sea, between Iran and Russia
SIZE	86,600 sq km, slightly smaller than Maine
POPULATION	7,868,385 (July 2004 est.)
INFANT MORTALITY	82.74 deaths/1,000 live births
THE PEOPLE	Azeri 90%, Dagestani 3.2%, Russian 2.5%, Armenian 2%, other 2.3%
RELIGIONS	Muslim 93.4%, Russian Orthodox 2.5%, Armenian Orthodox 2.3%, other 1.8%
LANGUAGES	Azerbaijani (Azeri) 89%, Russian 3%, Armenian 2%, other 6%
LITERACY RATE	Total population: 97% male: 99% female: 96%
GOVERNMENT	Republic
CAPITAL	Baku (Baki)

Rovshan Bagirov

Azerbaijan

28 years old, male, public relations and human resources specialist

Dear People of America,

I'm really worried about what is going on in the world vis-à-vis America. And I do fear that, as Americans, you will not understand what has happened. You may wonder why you are the target of hate and abuse in the future. I'm worried that some forces are interested in making America a weakened and unpopular nation.

During the war in Nagorno-Karabakh, I became friends with many Americans that came to assist Azerbaijani refugees that had fled from Armenia and Nagorno-Karabakh. I was able to see into their eyes and I observed the efforts of these people, who left their peaceful land of comfort. We had many conversations and made analyses about things in the world. We spoke of the problems of humankind, like what makes people kill each other? I still keep in touch with some of them. Those people create an image of respected and sensitive Americans—of a real people that are always ready to help. At the same time, there are politicians that are happy to create, at times, "artificial" grounds for Americans to take care somewhere in the world. I'm sure that my friends would stop the wars and bloodshed if they can and they'd never welcome those "artificial" reasons.

The work that they do in the world is filled with personal sacrifice and all that they are able to do to help others. I'm thankful to them and would wish to have more of this kind of patient constructors of peaceful life.

I'm sad to hear that the economic situation in the U.S. is slowly going down due to the events we observe. I think that the aggressive intention of your administration's latest international policy may bring opposite results and save your economy. But at what cost? The position of the U.S. in the world might melt down consequently. Let's hope for better.

The Iraq situation increases my daily concerns. Whatever happens now, we are all losers. It will take years to recover things in the Middle East, in Europe, and between the U.S. and so many of its (former?) allies.

I think that the aggressive intention of your administration's latest international policy may bring opposite results and save your economy. But at what cost?

As a child of the Soviet era, I'm familiar with what it means having only "black and white." At this time in history it seems that we have come to the point of believing that if one person gains we assume that another must loose. This can't be solved in the U.N. or anywhere else; it can only be solved with each of us individually. We need to look at what we are supporting. How do the daily decisions you make affect the rest of your world?

Things, as I can see from mass media reports, are rapidly changing the face of America. During the Soviet times, one who had an intention to criticize something, or define their own viewpoint regarding "things around" was supposed to be denigrated as the "homeland's enemy" or a provocateur. Seems that something similar has started in the Greatest Democracy of the World. I don't know the further attitude of Americans to the current changes (starting with the censorship in your free press). Are you aware of the great bias in your media?

I'm asking, why you believe that the only country empowered by the Almighty to define who is "good and evil" is the U.S.?

Americans like to believe that they are a Chosen People by God, accountable only to him. Of course, you also like to see yourselves as exceptional, with the right, even the duty, to be in breach of international codes and law. I'm asking, why you believe that the only country empowered by the Almighty to define who is "good and evil" is the U.S.? Doesn't it mean that you're trying to possess the ultimate truth (which is impossible)? As a result of such a "belief", the world (that repeatedly goes through the systematic route of historic mistakes) finds itself polarized. Here I'd just remind you of the Roman Empire. This polarization can bring more militant and violent consequences for our fragile world— already facing the threats of nuclear war. We observe the rise of radical, anti-Western Islamism, which is the result of several mental associations, whether justified or not: of Westernization (Americanization) with conspicuous consumption; of economic injustice; of faith with social redemption and political salvation. Probably all this helped to transform some Islamic movements into vehicles of radical insurgency against the regional regimes and against the American superpower that backs them, as they believe.

The conflict between colonialist and colony was not solved by compromise but by resistance. Resistance means to be active not only by arms, but also by a real desire to find the objective solution for future perspectives. As Prophet Muhammad (peace be upon him) said: "Help your brother, whether he is an oppressor or he is oppressed." People asked, "It is right to help him if he is oppressed, but how should we help him if he is an oppressor?" The Prophet said, "By preventing him from oppressing others."

A leader who has nothing better than "the conflicts between good and evil" and "the solution is to crush the evil," will not survive sustained questioning.

Here we can use the mind, knowledge and "tongue" pushed by Soul and heart to help each other.

Qur'an says: "When the Other shows an inclination toward peace that so do you; peace breeds peace. And the truth of zakat, of sharing with the poor." Sura 8:61.

Peace can be based on equality and equity, not only inside the U.S., but also between the U.S. and the outer world. From interpersonal violence there is a direct link to interstate wars. A leader who has nothing better than "the conflicts between good and evil" and "the solution is to crush the evil," will not survive sustained questioning. Except as war propaganda. Just to remind you: the former USSR had always been in search of enemies …

Equality as the basis of the law is a historical contribution to a culture of peace by the world nations. Exceptionalism is the opposite.

You, as Americans, have many privileged peculiarities, such as being naive, experiencing freedom, rights and pride for your country. But I would like to remind you that the truth can not be forced, even if it is the "American version of truth." Truth is a universal notion that shouldn't be brought on by tanks. Don't let some of your leaders import their blindness to each of your minds. Please don't let your administration repeat the mistakes of dead empires.

Rovshan Bagirov

Uzbekistan

WHERE	Central Asia, north of Afghanistan
SIZE	447,400 sq km, slightly larger than California
POPULATION	26,410,416 (July 2004 est.)
INFANT MORTALITY	71.3 deaths/1,000 live births
THE PEOPLE	Uzbek 80%, Russian 5.5%, Tajik 5%, Kazakh 3%, Karakalpak 2.5%, Tatar 1.5%, other 2.5%
RELIGIONS	Muslim 88% (mostly Sunnis), Eastern Orthodox 9%, other 3%
LANGUAGES	Uzbek 74.3%, Russian 14.2%, Tajik 4.4%, other 7.1%
LITERACY RATE	Total population: 99% male: 99.3% female: 99% (2003 est.)
GOVERNMENT	Republic; authoritarian presidential rule, with little power outside the executive branch
CAPITAL	Tashkent (Toshkent)

Saida Sultanaeva

Uzbekistan

22 years old, female, student of Oriental studies

We've got just one World
It's in our hands
Our world we've got to understand
The whole world—sea and land
One world in our hands …

Dear People of America,

What is America for me? A remote country of wonder? The land of freedom and happiness? Maybe it's just an illusion.

I'm twenty-two years old and a student from a country in Central Asia called Uzbekistan, one of the ex-Republic of USSR. Uzbekistan is where you can find huge plantations of cotton growing, where there is an abundance of sun and fruits, where the people are very tranquil and peaceful and do not hurry, where we are very proud of our ancestors, and love and respect their traditions and customs. I am representing Uzbek youth that is the majority of our nation. Sixty-five percent of the citizens in Uzbekistan are under age twenty-five.

Just like many American youths, I feel the wild desire to start my own new life. I want to be independent, to live separately of my family. I want to travel around the world, learn how people live in other nations, see other sides of the life by my own eyes!

I want to be free!

But! But I need a visa! Just a "small" and "simple" but unreachable formality which is very difficult to obtain. Only very rich people here have a chance to see the other countries; that's why more than half of the population have never been out of their home place and have never seen a plane. Before it was impossible because of the ideological reasons of USSR, but now it is because of economic reasons. This formality closes the frontiers in front of me, destroys my dreams, prevents me living as I want.

It makes me feel angry and desperate.

And I don't mean only America; to say simply, "poor" countries have a wall with "rich" countries. It's like two separate worlds. What do you think we feel watching the brilliance and allure of the MTV shows of Ricky Martin or Jennifer Lopez? How do you think we feel watching the super comfort, beautiful life, freedom in American Hollywood movies? Of course there is the natural desire to have the same. Why can Americans have this and not us? Why? We're not worse. Of course we all want to live well. And voila! The results of globalization: we can see it, but can't have it.

Maybe this is one of the reasons why we sometimes watch America with distrust and dislike. I think that today, when the processes of integration highly increase the economic, social, cultural and other levels, the actuality of rapprochement of nations is understood. People from different countries have to learn more about their neighbors, have to get to know closer the people that surround them. Who are they? How do they live? And not only through the television, but firstly by direct communication, by direct meeting of people. But all these "rapprochements" meet irresistible obstacles, like getting a visa.

Of course, opening of frontiers destroys the world system. What about national security, control of peoples' movement, the economic property of the nation? What about the inviolable frontiers—the unique culture of nations? But from the other side, these barriers lead into the disproportion of world development—some countries are "rich" some are "poor" and the distance between them increases more and more. When international relations only consider the interests of "rich" countries, it leads to inequality and injustice. And these contradictions of globalization have to be solved, because the most important thing is to prevent war.

Okay, to say truly, I used to imagine the ordinary American as a fatty with stupid and empty eyes, with chewing gum in the mouth, who doesn't care about anything and anybody—no intelligence, no manner, and of course, very proud of his country. But I changed my mind when some time ago my family rented our flat to a couple of Americans, Edwin and Nancy, who in fact were the contrary of my ideas. They were very thoughtful, open hearted, very kind and generous people. They lived in our apartment for two years and my family is very grateful and happy to know such people. I see now that every nation has its

...these contradictions of globalization have to be solved, because the most important thing is to prevent war.

I think that one of the most positive characteristics and advantages of American people is the spirit of toleration to the different ethnic societies...

own positive and negative sides. I think that one of the most positive characteristics and advantages of American people is the spirit of toleration to the different ethnic societies, confessions, convictions, and opinions within the country and toward the other nations of the world. For example, in ex-USSR the ethnic origin of a person always played a very important role—and unfortunately such attitude remains today in Uzbekistan. Getting to know someone new, firstly we pay usually too much attention to what is his ethnicity? Uzbek? Russian? Kazakh? Tatar? Jew? Because of the domination of different nationalities in different countries. And this makes lots of problems and tension between the relations of people. In United States everyone is American, not English, not Chinese. And the thought, "We are Americans" unites your nation; promotes ideas, "We're all equal!" "We are all together!"

Yes, America—the country of endless possibilities, high-level standard, where people can realize themselves and can get deserved salary for their work, the country of free behavior and norms where law works and you have real rights, and people know that their country protects them.

Here? What kind of opportunities do young people have? Unfortunately, not much: studying, marrying, or doing nothing, we can go work if we have a special relative or people to "push through." But even this way we know we won't get deserved money: in the best case, 25 dollars in a month. We can get more if we'll go just selling something in our markets. Many of my friends, after getting diplomas of higher education, have to stay selling something in the "Ippodrom," our biggest market. The dream to leave the country and earn some base capital is very popular among the Uzbeks. The biggest pride of any family is if one of the members is working or studying over there, somewhere in that gold world. This is not a sad story; this is reality.

Unfortunately, many of us young Uzbeks skeptically look at the idea of an economic miracle in Uzbekistan. We had lectures about the "National Ideology of Uzbekistan" and our teacher was proclaiming about "the progress of Uzbekistan during last ten years of independence, that we live in a democratic society, that she is satisfied by salary of 10 dollars in a month." The reaction was negative; laughing with irony and protesting. Students were thinking she is crazy. We aren't feeling any kind of enthusiasm about the great future of our country. It is very difficult to change the situation. Maybe first the world situation has to be changed?

I really do believe in a world without frontiers. …We all have to be more tolerant and wise, because we all live on one planet.

I really do believe in a world without frontiers. And that people can be happy not only in America, but all over the world. We all have to be more tolerant and wise, because we all live on one planet. America for me is a kind of mini example of the future's globe, a "mini world" with variety of cultures and peoples with different religions and opinions, where everybody is free and at the same time they have something in common. They have something that is uniting them—hope, belief, love, the sun, the land, the sky … the people.

Saida Sultanaeva

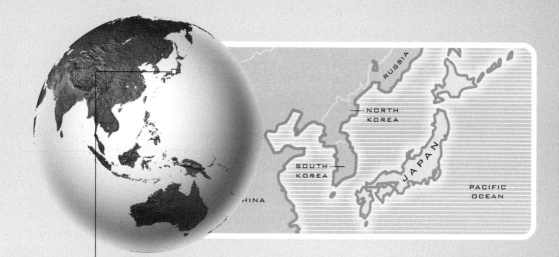

JAPAN

WHERE	Eastern Asia, island chain between the North Pacific Ocean and the Sea of Japan, east of the Korean Peninsula
SIZE	377,835 sq km *Note*: includes Bonin Islands (Ogasawara-gunto), Daito-shoto, Minami-jima, Okino-tori-shima, Ryukyu Islands (Nansei-shoto), and Volcano Islands (Kazan-retto), slightly smaller than California
POPULATION	127,333,002 (July 2004 est.)
INFANT MORTALITY	3.28 deaths/1,000 live births
THE PEOPLE	Japanese 99%, others 1% (Korean 511,262, Chinese 244,241, Brazilian 182,232, Filipino 89,851, other 237,914)
RELIGIONS	Observe both Shinto and Buddhist 84%, other 16% (including Christian 0.7%)
LANGUAGES	Japanese
LITERACY RATE	Total population: 99%
GOVERNMENT	Constitutional monarchy with a parliamentary government
CAPITAL	Tokyo

Aya Ikeda

Japan
27 years old, female, ceramic artist

Dear People of America,

Your country America is very familiar to me as I stayed there twice before. The reason I went to America was because I simply felt I must have a look at this amazing country. I think your country America has something that really attracts the rest of us. It's probably because your people have the spirit of freedom and it gives us opportunity to have our dreams come true.

I was enthusiastic about American movies at that time. American movies embody a creative spirit, and I imagined this might be true of the people. From the movies, I had a kind of a vision about the people living there. For me, they seemed jolly, shiny and powerful people. So, I finally couldn't resist myself going to visit the United States.

My first stay was in Santa Monica, California. It was just great! I would never forget the days I spent there. I saw many weird but nice people. It was just like being in an American movie. And I enjoyed it so much! I loved people-watching! I saw a black bus driver who was driving the bus while eating doughnuts! And he was also singing rap music, and as the bus stop was getting closer, he'd tell us the name of the bus stop with singing as

lyrics. I was just so happy on this bus. Also, I saw the man with a "music note" shape tattoo on his neck. And there was a girl wearing a red sweater even though it was a red-hot summer! She had a hand-made bag—also red—and the cloth was like her sweater. This is part of the weird people I saw. I was so happy to know that these people exist in your country. Our countries are very different.

I know those things would be a usual matter for your people. But I'm sure it wouldn't be happening in my homeland, Japan. I always felt my country is quite strict. Everything goes on with rules. People are afraid of what other people think of you. So everyone tries to be the same in order to feel safe in the group. I've heard Japanese companies prefer to hire the person who's good at cooperation rather than who's creative and who has new ideas. This is also telling you what kind of society we have. Your country America would be opposite from this, I can imagine. And I think kind of the attitude Japan has, is just like making good soldiers or robots who'll just obey what they are told to do. Actually, as you know, Japan had a famous "kamikaze pilots" at the War time. They were sort of robots who died for the nation.

I think America is the place that odd people can exist as they are. The freedom that your country has is a very respectable thing.

Also Japan likes to copy things from other countries. I cannot imagine America copying things from other countries. Your country seems to have their own way to deal with things and new ideas which always surprise us. I think America is the place that

162

odd people can exist as they are. The freedom that your country has is a very respectable thing.

Some people in other countries might feel your government is interfering with their culture and traditions with America's foreign policy. This is only my conjecture, but many of the countries would prefer America to not interfere with them, as American people would not want this interference by others. For example, if another country came over to America and decided that your people should not enjoy paintings from now on because they think that's the right thing to do in life, you would definitely object to this. You should not allow your government to change other countries to be like yours.

In Japan, young people admire your country America. I think because America has attractive culture and geography. But the older generation, I cannot say they are fond of your country. It's probably because they know about the War period and the atomic bombs which destroyed two parts of Japan altogether. People there are still suffering disease from the radioactivity and will never forget what Americans did to them. I lately watched the documentary about Japan in the War period. They showed a video taken by an American solder with his movie camera. One Japanese woman with a baby dropped herself and the baby into the sea from the cliff. And this was happening when the woman saw the American soldiers coming towards her. Do you have any idea why she threw herself into the deep sea? Japanese civilians were told that "American's are devils. If they get you, they will

This is only my conjecture, but many of the countries would prefer America to not interfere with them, as American people would not want this interference by others.

eat you." It is very sad that many people believed this. And the tragedy happened all over Japan. People in Japan had no idea what Americans are like, as we'd been in "national isolation" for a long time. What is more, they believed that chocolate was made out of blood. They were believing that our nation was winning the war against America because the Japanese government was lying through the radio.

I've heard that's why America dropped the atomic bombs to stop the silly War.

But also I've heard that they just wanted to try the power of their atomic bombs. I don't know which was the truth, but one thing I surely know is that it is not right to drop the atomic bomb on the place full of civilians and destroy the culture in just a few seconds. No matter what kind of reason they had, this is not right. There are many countries in this world and we should admire each other's own cultures and traditions that we are proud of. And develop our countries together, rather than destroy or interfere with one another.

As you know, we are all different as individuals and nations. So try to understand and communicate with each other. It is very important. I'm not talking only about American and Japanese people, any other countries that are in this world.

And we should always remember the saying "two wrongs do not make a right."

Best regards to the American people!

Aya Ikeda

There are many countries in this world and we should admire each other's own cultures and traditions that we are proud of.

CHINA

WHERE	Eastern Asia, bordering the South and East China Seas and Yellow Sea, between North Korea and Vietnam
SIZE	9,596,960 sq km, slightly smaller than the U.S.
POPULATION	1,284,303,705
INFANT MORTALITY	27.25 deaths/1,000 live births
THE PEOPLE	Han Chinese 91.9%, Zhuang, Uygur, Hui, Yi, Tibetan, Miao, Manchu, Mongol, Buyi, Korean, and others 8.1%
RELIGIONS	Taoist, Buddhist, Muslim 1%–2%, Christian 3%–4% *Note:* officially atheist
LANGUAGES	Standard Chinese or Mandarin (Beijing dialect), Yue (Cantonese), Wu (Shanghaiese), Minbei (Fuzhou), Minnan (Hokkien-Taiwanese), Xiang, Gan, Hakka dialects
LITERACY RATE	Total population: 81.5% male: 89.9% female: 72.7%
GOVERNMENT	Communist state
CAPITAL	Beijing

Sun Xiao Fei

China

23 years old, male, studying marine navigation

Dear People of America,

When I was very little, the story of America was given to me by my old uncle who was a veteran of the Korean War. He told me that America was the war-maker in the world. The earth would never be in peace with its existence. I was deeply impressed by his frightening words.

My bad impression of America was not changed until one of my close friends left me. At my age of sixteen, my desk mate, also my bosom friend, moved to America with his father who was an acute businessman. From then on, more and more people around me went abroad for America. But few of them came back again.

I began to doubt my beliefs. As people I knew connected with other people in America, I began to understand more about why anyone would want to live in this land thought to be so destructive. The reason lies in the high quality of life in America. While most Chinese go to work by bikes, cars have been part of America for decades. It is a world of difference, and to most Chinese, America is a country of opportunity with things that they haven't even dreamed of.

A few years after, I met Karl, my first foreign teacher from America—

a very well-read man. In contrast to my Chinese teachers, Karl preferred to live independently. Our college offers every teacher a three-week vacation per year. Most Chinese teachers would rather take it together as a group while Karl went alone every time. While Karl enjoyed his time I think maybe he will never encounter the happiness that the Chinese teachers share as a group which rested on the basis of the collective and not an individual.

As a Chinese, I never loose my wonder of America—a country which is loved by quite a lot of people including my desk mate's family and hated by others such as my old uncle. The reason may be something like this: America is the only super nation in the world. With a solid foundation in economy, it can provide a wonderful atmosphere for investors all over the world. It is reliable to build a "rags to riches" story. And its dependable character helps.

Since America is the most powerful nation in the world, its future will severely affect other nations.

Every blade has two sides. Despite America's prosperous business and ambitious culture, the nation has run into ignorance of other peoples. In America, the world is monopolized by one language, one culture, one thought. The entry of any others proves to be very difficult. Since the entry is very difficult, communication becomes even more difficult.

What's worst is that ignorance often leads to misunderstanding. To set against the ignorance, China can be taken as a model. We begin to learn English from Junior-One in middle school and continue to study English throughout high school. Plus, over the past twenty years, China has set up hundreds of language-training schools teaching English and other foreign languages as well. This action has been convenient for many overseas investors and earned benefits for us.

Since America is the most powerful nation in the world, its future will severely affect other nations. So I believe a more friendly and flourishing America will take the fancy of the people all over the world. I think only by means of cooperation, the world will live in peace forever—a world where my old uncle and American veterans have never lived.

God Bless America. God Bless our peoples.

Yours truly,

Sun Xiao Fei

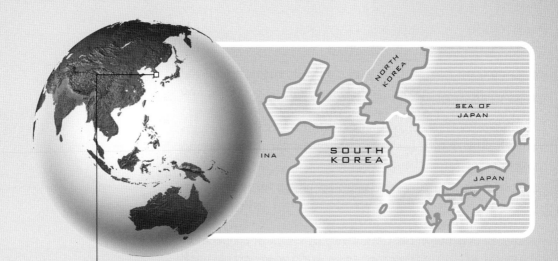

SOUTH KOREA

WHERE	Eastern Asia, southern half of the Korean Peninsula bordering the Sea of Japan and the Yellow Sea
SIZE	98,480 sq km, slightly larger than Indiana
POPULATION	48,598,175 (July 2004 est.)
INFANT MORTALITY	7.18 deaths/1,000 live births
THE PEOPLE	Homogeneous (except for about 20,000 Chinese)
RELIGIONS	Christian 49%, Buddhist 47%, Confucianist 3%, Shamanist, Chondogyo (Religion of the Heavenly Way), and other 1%
LANGUAGES	Korean, English widely taught in junior high and high school
LITERACY RATE	Total population: 98.1% male: 99.3% female: 97% (2003 est.)
GOVERNMENT	Republic
CAPITAL	Seoul

Yu-Jin Kim

South Korea

18 years old, female, high school student

Dear People of America,

I'm writing because I have a favor to ask you. You might think it's a big favor but maybe when you hear my story, it will help you understand why I ask. Maybe this letter will help you understand my country better.

My name is Yu-Jin. I live in the southwestern part of South Korea, Gwangju. I am a second-year high school student that studies all day and night at school six days a week. My home to me often feels like a sleeping bag since my family is usually already asleep by the time I come home. Rarely do I get to see them, but when I do have a chance I like to spend my time with family, especially with my grandmother.

My grandmother's sister, Soon-ae Kim, lives in North Korea. I haven't seen her, but I have heard about her from my grandmother. I haven't met her, but I dream of the day. Soon-ae and my grandmother separated from each other after the Korean War in 1950 and they haven't been able to meet each other since. After the war, Korea was divided into two countries, South Korea and North Korea. At that time, my grandmother was about twenty years old, she is now over seventy. She stayed here in South Korea with her other sister and brother, but one sister was left behind in North Korea. So they could not see each other anymore. My grandmother has missed her sister for a very long time.

171

I remember how much she misses her. When I was a child, she cried when she told me about her sister. At that time, I couldn't understand why she couldn't meet her. I'd ask, "Grandma, why are you crying? Do you miss your sister? If you miss her then why don't you go there and see her?" I tried to console her, but now I think I just gave her more pain.

There have been a few opportunities for separated families like my grandmothers to meet their lost relatives in the North, but they are extremely difficult to do. My grandmother wasn't one of the lucky ones. She just cried when she watched on TV other families reunite for only a few hours before they had to go back to their own homes. I was sad when watching this because I couldn't do anything to help my grandmother. I know she still misses her. Now I want to meet her. We don't know each other but we are family and I love her very much.

Many of us Korean people, including myself, are really worried that North Korea will be another Iraq.

These days, there are many problems in North Korea. The most important problem is the nuclear weapons issue. Because of this, America, South Korea, Japan, Russia, and China are trying to work together to solve the problem. The United States and South Korea are especially trying to persuade North Korea to stop making nuclear weapons, but North Korea doesn't listen. So America is angry now.

Many of us Korean people, including myself, are really worried that North Korea will be another Iraq. This rumor frightens us. I know that there is probably little possibility of America going to war with North Korea, but if they do, so many innocent victims in the North will be killed. So I ask you to please solve this issue peacefully. Though the North Korean leader, Kim Jong-II, doesn't listen we should still not go to war because it would only make matters worse. Instead I believe there should be many talks among all the surrounding countries. We should try to communicate with the North.

In North Korea, there are many innocent and poor people. One of them is part of my family. Just as you in America love your family and wouldn't want anything to happen to them, I also don't want anything to happen to mine. I'm not sure if my grandmother's sister is still alive, but I hope so. I pray for my grandmother to stay healthy so that someday I can bring her to see Soon-ae in North Korea. This is my dream.

Maybe through reading my story you'll be able to gain a better understanding of the people in my country. I ask the American people to please not forget that North Koreans are people just like the ones in your families. I hope one day North and South Korea will be reunited and I'll be able to meet my family in North Korea. But first let's solve the problems with the North peacefully. I ask you to do your best to work for peace.

Your friend,

Yu-Jin Kim

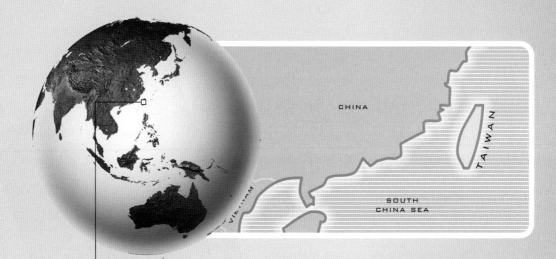

TAIWAN

WHERE	Eastern Asia, islands bordering the East China Sea, Philippine Sea, South China Sea, and Taiwan Strait, north of the Philippines, off the southeastern coast of China
SIZE	35,980 sq km, slightly smaller than Maryland and Delaware combined
POPULATION	22,749,838 (July 2004 est.)
INFANT MORTALITY	6.52 deaths/1,000 live births
THE PEOPLE	Taiwanese (including Hakka) 84%, mainland Chinese 14%, aborigine 2%
RELIGIONS	Buddhist, Confucian, and Taoist 93%, Christian 4.5%, other 2.5%
LANGUAGES	Mandarin Chinese (official), Taiwanese (Min), Hakka dialects
LITERACY RATE	Total population: 94% (2004 est.)
GOVERNMENT	Multiparty democratic regime headed by popularly elected president and unicameral legislature
CAPITAL	Taipei

Yen-Wen Vivian Chen

TAIWAN
26 YEARS OLD, FEMALE, RESEARCHER AT THE CHILD
WELFARE LEAGUE FOUNDATION

Dear People of America,

Greetings from Taiwan! I spent two years studying at NYU for the master's degree and came back to work in the Child Welfare League Foundation in Taiwan. According to my personal experiences, I would like to share my point of view about your country and the differences between the U.S. and Taiwan.

Generally speaking, people in Taiwan get impressions of America through TV programs and Hollywood movies. Therefore, the image of American we perceive would mostly be the lifestyle of the American middle class—easy, abundant, independent, and enjoying leisure time. The close relationship between Taiwan and America cannot be overstated. There are lots of Taiwanese people traveling to U.S. According to the statistics, there are averagely 275,000 non-immigrants traveling from Taiwan to the U.S. each year, for the past ten years. There are economic, political, and marital relationships between America and Taiwan as well. Most of Taiwan's people get impression of Americans as friendly, straightforward, and pragmatic people with sense of justice. On the other hand, we also realize that the American government is self-benefit oriented, especially in economic and political issues.

My parents own a small company and make export trading business with Americans; therefore my sister and I have had many chances to meet with my parents' clients. When I was a little girl, I like when those American clients came to visit because I would have the opportunity to go to the high-class restaurants to have ice cream which I was not allowed to have normally. Moreover, these American uncles were nice and funny. I thank my parents a lot because they took these chances as social contact lessons and showed me manners of dining and conversations. They also taught me to learn from their sense of humor and encouraged me to widen my viewpoints so that I would have diverse topics of conversation for social occasions. They also asked me to be myself.

The learning styles are extremely different between America and Taiwan. I would see American students raise their hands asking questions frequently in class. This is because American students are encouraged to participate regardless of what they offer. Well, if you ask me, I would honestly tell you that some of the questions are silly ones. (Sorry, please forgive me. I know that Rule Number One in the American classroom is, "no stupid questions!") They got high grades because of their "aggressive participation," which at first makes no sense to me. I couldn't be convinced that asking questions without processing with their head equals benefit. I was taught to ask "reasonable questions" when needed, and, after thinking. On the other hand, I cannot say which learning style is better because different learning styles create different advantages.

Creativity, for example, is one of the advantages of American learning style; while the learning style in Taiwan trains students to process the information in a short time and it's better-off in math and science.

The Big Apple is one of the most modern cities in the world, and so is Taipei city, where I grew up. The lifestyle and the pace of the people are pretty much the same in these two cities. However, the thing I missed most when I was in N.Y. was Taiwanese food. Generally speaking, we have our dinner with three to five dishes, and eat with rice. The dishes usually include vegetables, meat or fish, and egg or tofu. We usually have soup after the dishes. After the meal, fruit or dessert are served. Here, I am talking about the daily dinner in average families in Taiwan. While in U.S., a regular meal seems to be a main course, with potatoes, mostly. And vegetables are served as side dishes. Moreover, when talking about American culture, I believe the first thing that bombs into most people's head would be a big hamburger. For my personal taste, Western foods are way too simple and with too many raw or cold dishes.

I have also experienced a great impact from my work. The Child Welfare League Foundation, where I work, provides various kinds of services to children and their families, one of which is an adoption service. In Taiwan, blood relationship is highly valued. This is a major obstacle in promoting adoption based on love instead of blood. People in Taiwan do not prefer adopting older kids because they would know that the adopted family is not original family, not even talking about children with some physical issues to deal with. However, we have had abandoned children adopted by Americans, who are mostly older kids that cannot be accepted by Taiwan's families. There was a ten-year-old boy who was an "old" client in our organization. He was abandoned and could not find an appropriate adopted family. Not only because he was an older child but he had some behavioral and emotional issues resulting from his difficult life experiences. He came into our office for game therapy periodically. I felt very bad for him, because his misbehavior is understandable and he desired a family of his own. He had suffered a lot compared with the kids at his age. I can understand that it takes a world of courage for anyone to adopt a kid like him. After all, adoption is a lifetime commitment. After a few years of waiting, there was an American family came into the boy's life. They adopted him, they love him and treat him like the angel that he is. They tolerate his temper and take it as tests, and teach him with clear principles and great patience. I am truly touched by this great love. I do think that the spirit of philanthropy is much more common in America than in Taiwan. Therefore, in the perspective of open-mindedness and caring for children rights, I really admire Americans.

I think one should cherish and understand his/her own culture, and this should be the first priority.

I am lucky to have had two years in America and get to know its culture, in a close way. I am also happy to have this chance to share Taiwan's culture with you. I feel that it is important to cherish what we possess. We are in an era of Internet and globalization. We have more and more opportunities to see how people live in the rest of the world. I think one should cherish and understand his/her own culture, and this should be the first priority. After knowing one's own culture, s/he will have the ability to appreciate others'. Taiwan is a very small island (1390 square miles, smaller than Delaware State) with

We are part of a global village. We have responsibilities to protect and appreciate the diversity in this village.

23 million people. Therefore, you can imagine how Taiwanese parents value "competitive advantages" when educating their kids. I cannot deny that American culture is the mainstream in the world, but I would disagree that we should raise Taiwan's children in the American way, not before they get to know their homeland and Taiwan's culture. We are part of a global village. We have responsibilities to protect and appreciate the diversity in this village. It would be a positive step if the people of the world would agree to support each other in the protection of our cultural heritage.

Vivian

SOUTHEAST ASIA

LAOS

CAMBODIA

MALAYSIA

BRUNEI

M. Brecke

LAOS

WHERE	Southeastern Asia, northeast of Thailand, west of Vietnam
SIZE	236,800 sq km, slightly larger than Utah
POPULATION	6,068,117 (July 2004 est.)
INFANT MORTALITY	87.06 deaths/1,000 live births
THE PEOPLE	Lao Loum (lowland) 68%, Lao Theung (upland) 22%, Lao Soung (highland) including the Hmong ("Meo") and the Yao (Mien) 9%, ethnic Vietnamese/Chinese 1%
RELIGIONS	Buddhist 60%, animist and other 40% (including various Christian denominations 1.5%)
LANGUAGES	Lao (official), French, English, and various ethnic languages
LITERACY RATE	Total population: 52.8% male: 67.5% female: 38.1% (2003 est.)
GOVERNMENT	Communist state
CAPITAL	Vientiane

KONG KEO

LAOS

24 YEARS OLD, MALE, GUEST HOUSE OWNER AND
TOUR GUIDE

Dear People of America,

I was raised in a poor village. Every day, starting at six years old, I helped my parents work because every child has to. This may sound like a very different life than America, but in my village in Laos we never had a lonely life. We were always working together and were very happy.

I think the country America has affected me mostly because of the war. You may think I mean the Vietnam War, but I mean the secret war in Laos. Most people in the world misunderstand and they think that the war in Laos is the same war. But they are different. For nine years, U.S. dropped more than two million tons of bombs here because of communism in Southeast Asia. It is called the secret war because not many people knew about it.

I was born after the war, but many people say that the war is not finished yet because still many people get killed every day. Still they get hurt every day, because there are so many bombs left over here. My mom told me like every eight minutes a plane came to put the bomb to the village—napalm bomb. Everyone had to move, and leave to the jungle. For example, my parents lived for eight or nine years in a tunnel, so they forget what sticky rice looks like. In this time they can't come to the village to find the rice, they have to hide

M. Brecke

These days I am scared for my culture because of what I learn and see. Now is tourism time in Laos. Tourism is good for the economy but we lose the culture.

in the tunnel and be hungry. They looked for potatoes in the jungle or banana flower. The tunnel is still there. I go back there with them to visit sometimes; they respect the tunnel. They believe that the tunnel saved their life until the war finished. When they have a holiday they bring offerings to the spirits there.

When I was young in the village, I will never forget one terrible day. With my friends after school we were playing around an old American cluster bomb that we found and we didn't know. That day my dad gave curfew and I went early to help my mom with work. I left and then the bomb exploded and killed a couple of my friends and four of them got hurt by this bomb, big hurt. I can say that the war has made a lot of hurt to my heart. You can see the villagers get killed by the bombs every year. I feel hate for America as well. I hate because the villagers did nothing to America; they only live their life in the village, and they want to have a long life but they don't have one because they get killed.

Sometimes when I see American tourists traveling to this area, the villagers sometime want to ask something and the American tourist, not all of them, they think they are too high class to talk with them, like they are the hero. This makes me feel not nice to America. A lot of the villagers in the area feel bad like that also. Americans just think the American way is right all of the time. When they stay in my guest house, they complain because they always compare to the one in the States. It's hard to tell what I should say to help them understand the difference in our cultures.

I look and see how the whole world is changing, like the Internet. A very convenient, fast life—so fast people don't need to lose sweat. I don't know what will happen to humans because they don't need to work. For example, to mail, they don't need to carry the letters. I don't know what the people, what the bodies will be like when they don't need to move. For me, if I don't walk or exercise I don't feel very good.

These days I am scared for my culture because of what I learn and see. Now is tourism time in Laos. Tourism is good for the economy but we lose the culture. Americans should learn our culture, but we need to keep the culture as well. For example, in Vang Vienne, the culture used to be very nice, but now it's not so nice. Before, every woman had to wear the sarong, a long skirt, and when they walk past people they had to lower their head. But now it's very hard to see something like that. Many Lao people follow the fashion of the West, the tight shirt, you see it quite often.

"You have to look to the mirror to see what your face looks like." You should look before you say you always do good.

I want to say to Americans, I have never been in the United States. I don't know what America looks like, but from what I heard this is a big country. So maybe the people don't know if the government did something wrong to Laos. In Laos we have the idiom: "You have to look to the mirror to see what your face looks like." You should look before you say you always do good. Are you always true? Always do the right thing? That is what I want you to let American people know.

Kong Keo

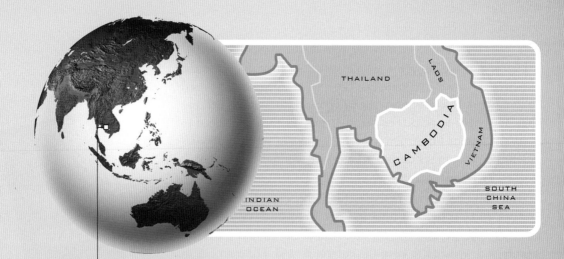

CAMBODIA

WHERE	Southeastern Asia, bordering the Gulf of Thailand, between Thailand, Vietnam, and Laos
SIZE	181,040 sq km, slightly smaller than Oklahoma
POPULATION	13,363,421
INFANT MORTALITY	73.67 deaths/1,000 live births (2004 est.)
THE PEOPLE	Khmer 90%, Vietnamese 5%, Chinese 1%, other 4%
RELIGIONS	Theravada Buddhist 95%, other 5%
LANGUAGES	Khmer (official) 95%, French, English
LITERACY RATE	Total population: 69.9% male: 80.5% female: 60.3% (2003 est.)
GOVERNMENT	Multiparty democracy under a constitutional monarchy established in September 1993
CAPITAL	Phnom Penh

Veasna Chea

CAMBODIA

29 YEARS OLD, FEMALE, HUMAN RIGHTS ASSISTANT AT
COHCHR, MEMBER OF CAMBODIA BAR ASSOCIATION

Dear People of America,

As a Cambodian, I am amazed at the opportunities that American people have. These opportunities you take for granted while we are working very hard toward them. I am amazed by your luck of the fact that you were born and live in a prosperous, transparent, and democratic society with a strong government. I view America as an ideal place to live.

Unlike American people, both my family and I, as well as other Cambodian people, suffered through decades of war that resulted from ideological influences—communism versus democracy—and national extremist leaders. For example, many bombs were dropped in many places in Cambodia by America to destroy the communist movement when the American government supported the Cambodian democratic leadership of General Lon Nol in the 1970s. As a result, many innocent Cambodian people died, among them five of my close relatives. People at that time were very insecure; every house had a bunker. They heard people get killed every day. In my family, my great grandfather had six girls and one son. The son, my uncle, got hit by the blast of a bomb one day and passed away a day later. All the family has been grieving since then, especially my grandfather and his six sisters, of which one is my mother. She keeps talking how great he was. His death was recalled again when my grandfather passed away. As part of the Chinese tradition, only the son could hold the incense. My grandfather knew in advance of this problem and was sorry and worried for thirty years for the fact that he would not have somebody to take care of this duty. In addition, during the war with Vietnam, America dropped so many bombs in Cambodia that it traumatized the Cambodian people who live in the provinces along the Vietnamese border enough to feel like it was a war in Cambodia. Many temples and public institutions were destroyed or ruined. I feel so sad that all of our treasures, the heart of every Cambodian, were destroyed—and I wonder why we deserved this destruction and for what reason could be justified this bombardment.

Besides this, Cambodian people and my family lived through more than three years in the Killing Fields regime led by the Khmer Rouge, which tortured and killed 1.7 million people, including my father, who was taken away and killed when I was two years old. I was too young to remember everything, but what I can remember is that my mom did not allow us to cry or to show our sadness to the Ang Ka for our safety. When it happened, my brother, who was working in the field far away from us heard about my father being taken and ran for many miles, swam across streams and rivers to meet my mother. He went out and asked many soldiers about the fate of my father and finally he was guided to the place where my father was executed. At midnight, my mother and my eight sisters and brothers walked to the ditch where my father's corpse was left. My second brother went down and searched for the corpse. What

I can vaguely remember was the soft and bloody corpse of my father in the hands of my second brother. We took him in the middle of the night to avoid the eyes of the Ang Ka to a place near a pagoda and buried him in Kampong Spue Province. We now visit his grave regularly once a year. I feel that innocent Cambodian people are very unfortunate to have lived in a regime led by the most cruel dictator. It is the failure of the international community allowing this to happen without intervention.

Despite the suffering that Cambodian people received from America in the past, many Cambodians now are still pro-American.

I now still wonder whether the American people and government knew about these events? If yes, why did they fail to persuade the world to end that regime like they have done now in Iraq? Or they have two different policies?

Despite the suffering that Cambodian people received from America in the past, many Cambodians now are still pro-American. They believe that America played some role in bringing democracy to Cambodia in 1993. Many Cambodian people in particular love listening to Voice of America (VOA) radio. They love listening to speakers talk about democracy, freedom, and true information about Cambodia. I remember over ten years ago my grandfather, who was eighty years old at that time, would get up every morning at five a.m. to listen to VOA. One day, he heard the speech of President Bush (the father) about the possible change of regime in Cambodia at that time. He used his two-palms to pray and greet in a Cambodian way to the radio and said, "Please help Cambodian people,

Sir." He was very pleased that finally the United Nations came into Cambodia in 1993. He died at the age of ninety-two in January 2000 with the first hope that his grandchildren would enjoy peace and democracy and that his grandchildren won't go through war for a whole life like him (France, Japan, America, Vietnam, and civil war).

Now, many Cambodian people still think that they don't live in a true democratic country and some are still hoping that the American government will help them in democracy in Cambodia. They want to speak out, but they are afraid. Recently, my American friend and I went to an island on the Mekong River named Koh Dach to spend our weekend day at the beach. The area is famous for weaving silk underneath each house with large wooden looms. Both men and women weave all day for $1 in income each. We entered into a house where an elder couple was busy weaving, and they stopped and talked to us. The man asked my American friend "Where are you from?" to which he answered, "from America." The old man then said, "Oh, I'm very happy to meet you. American, I want to tell you something. We Cambodian people have not yet enjoyed true democracy. We are still afraid. We are so poor and our public institutions are very corrupt." He continued, "I would like to send a message to the American people and government", while pointing to pictures of President George W. Bush and Secretary of State Colin Powell that appeared in a local newspaper on the topic of the Iraq war. "Cambodian people want them to help us like they have helped the Iraqi people." My American friend said

Cambodian people want them to help us like they have helped the Iraqi people.

the issue in Cambodia is not as sensitive to Americans as is Iraq. To this the old couple replied, "Cambodian issues have never been viewed as sensitive by America, even during the Khmer Rouge regime. Cambodian people have had enough with war. We all have scars from the wars and have experienced that war is very bad. But I tell you, living in the dictatorial regime is perhaps even worse."

In the meantime, many Cambodians appreciate and acknowledge the American efforts through many aid agencies in Cambodia. Unfortunately, the Cambodian people need more help and care from their own government as well as the international community. With the hope that America and international communities will continue to support and promote democracy in Cambodia, Cambodian people hope that one day to live in a free and peaceful country and able to escape poverty like American people.

Veasna Chea

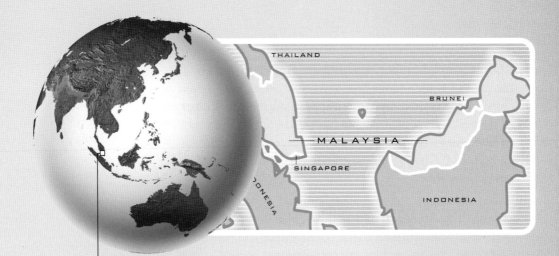

MALAYSIA

WHERE	Southeastern Asia, peninsula and northern one-third of the island of Borneo, bordering Indonesia and the South China Sea, south of Vietnam
SIZE	329,750 sq km, slightly larger than New Mexico
POPULATION	23,522,482 (July 2004 est.)
INFANT MORTALITY	18.35 deaths/1,000 live births
THE PEOPLE	Malay and other indigenous 58%, Chinese 24%, Indian 8%, others 10%
RELIGIONS	Muslim, Buddhist, Daoist, Hindu, Christian, Sikh; *Note—* in addition, Shamanism is practiced in East Malaysia
LANGUAGES	Bahasa Melayu (official), English, Chinese dialects (Cantonese, Mandarin, Hokkien, Hakka, Hainan, Foochow), Tamil, Telugu, Malayalam, Panjabi, Thai
LITERACY RATE	Total population: 88.9% male: 92.4% female: 85.4% (2003 est.)
GOVERNMENT	Constitutional monarchy
CAPITAL	Kuala Lumpur

WAN SAUDISANI

MALAYSIA
24 YEARS OLD, MALE, MEDICAL STUDENT

Dear People of America,

My friends call me Wan. Wan, in Malay history, represents dignities in the Malay Sultanate. Nowadays, anyone could use Wan in front of their names. You can call me anything that you feel comfortable.

I am a Malay-Chinese descendant. I live in Kelantan, Malaysia. Right now I am doing a medical course at the local university. The degree takes about seven years to complete. It is quite boring if you have no interest in medicine. I am also interested in language. Languages are important when it comes to making friends. I am fluent in our Malay language and English. At the moment, I am learning Arabic, Thai, French, Mandarin, and Cantonese. I love to make friends from many different cultures. I hope we can be friends. Friendship is something that is hard to describe, but whatever your culture or age, I will accept you as you are.

The U.S. means a lot to me and Malaysians. She brings investments to Malaysia and gives me and our people work. More work for our people means more money comes into the country. I am familiar with your life, your food, your books, etc. Everything that you have, we try to bring it here. We have got a place here that emulates a sidewalk café like most American famous cafés. Everyone here likes to be in there. If this is a good or bad

influence depends on the individual's view to maintain our own values or mix up globalization into life. I think the local tradition needs to be maintained; if not, we will not be true Malaysians.

Malaysia is multi-racial country which consists of Malays, Chinese, Indian, and numerous indigenous groups such as the Ibans, Dayaks, Kadazans, Bidayuhs, and Muruts. Integration, which has been nurtured through tolerance and respect for one another, is evident in the celebration of festivals—religious or ethnic. Malaysian culture is a healthy mix of diverse distinct cultures, its own indigenous practices intermingle with Islamic, Chinese, Indian, and Western values. This has brought about a fascinating potpourri of customs, songs, and dances.

Most people in the world have been influenced by your values. Your country is the best place in the world, where we look to for a reference for everything. It has moved in on us in stages for years. Suddenly, the new generation likes to eat American fast food rather than our own exotic Asian food. It is something that was inevitable, but the old generation still strongly holds onto our roots. They might not understand why this beloved country is not a virgin anymore, but most people have been infiltrated by foreign values that were not here fifty years ago. I admit that I go out and eat all American foods once in while. To eat it is not a problem when you know why you eat it. A problem will arise if I eat it a lot because the food is designed for a non-tropical country, so I need to watch out.

We emulate everything from U.S. Why? The U.S. acts as the father of all nations in the world. The third world watches the father through the windows of television, the Internet, movies, music, food, and almost everything. Even the local programs try to mimic American ways, which looks so weird when I look at it. I think you would be surprised to see the American style of comedy in our local television shows. Maybe none of you realize that as our older generation is replaced by a new generation, we are becoming an Americanized nation. In other words, we have embraced the feeling of what it is to be a developed nation, even though we are still developing.

I give my condolences to your community for the hideous events of September 11. I grieve for you and with you. Real Muslims should know that killing innocent people is totally wrong. However, the reaction of the U.S. government was unaccepted by the Malaysian people. The impact of the reaction has increased Islamophobia and attacks against well-behaved Muslims. Now, two Muslim countries have been attacked by the American administration due to causes that were not reasonable and logical.

We have embraced the feeling of what it is to be a developed nation, even though we are still developing.

We use U.S. dollars as our currency of trading. We try to see how a developed country manages their country. It looks like a utopian nation. That is why we try to be like the U.S. in every aspect of life, even though it looks awkward. Maybe by doing what the Americans do it will make us developed faster.

Wan

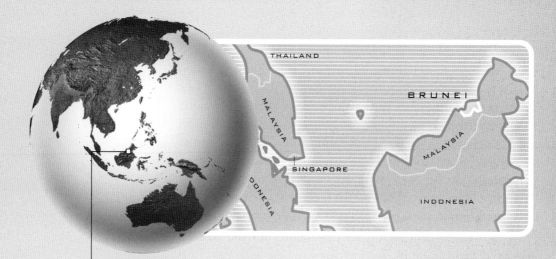

BRUNEI

WHERE	Southeastern Asia, bordering the South China Sea and Malaysia
SIZE	5,770 sq km, slightly smaller than Delaware
POPULATION	365,251 (July 2004 est.)
INFANT MORTALITY	13.05 deaths/1,000 live births
THE PEOPLE	Malay 67%, Chinese 15%, indigenous 6%, other 12%
RELIGIONS	Muslim (official) 67%, Buddhist 13%, Christian 10%, indigenous beliefs and other 10%
LANGUAGES	Malay (official), English, Chinese
LITERACY RATE	Total population: 91.8% male: 94.8% female: 88.5% (2003 est.)
GOVERNMENT	Constitutional sultanate
CAPITAL	Bandar Seri Begawan

VANESSA FERROLINO

BRUNEI

18 YEARS OLD, FEMALE, HIGH SCHOOL STUDENT

Dear People of America,

I am writing from Brunei. I am a Filipino citizen, but was born and raised here. Life here is considerably different from that of the Philippines or anywhere else, mostly because Brunei is a Muslim country. But having grown up here my whole life, I have learned to appreciate and adjust to its culture. There are no clubs, no nightlife, alcohol is banned, and even casual kissing in public is a punishable offense. This does not bother me at all because to me, these are just a few of the many sources of crime and disorder, which America faces every day. To many, they are essentials in life. America declares that it offers "everything," yet people wake up to predictable dangers every day. America cannot compare to the peace and tranquility that Brunei offers.

While Brunei adheres to strict Islamic conduct, the American influence on youth is pronounced. Clothes, music, and even the accent is imitated. Due to Islamic virtues, however, people are refrained from expressing sexuality and using foul language in public, which are quite normal in your society. I am glad that that is not the case here, because it is a pity that as generations and the new century progress, America feels even freer in exposing vulgarities—especially through the big screen. Children everywhere inevitably learn from it. It teaches them to become disrespectful and indecent. From my experience, I know that it induces morally violating thoughts that lead to corrupt actions. For example, pre-marital sex seems so normal in America next to smoking weed and homicide. This is not the kind of society in which a moral example could be set. Our part of the world is neither old-fashioned nor conservative; we simply keep to our moral values so that children grow up to be contented, proud, and worthy individuals.

Television is the gateway to America. When I was very young, movies inspired me to dream of residing in America and leading an all-American way of life. I was envious of the riches and glamour accentuated by your country. But as I grew older and I became more aware of the realities, my thoughts changed. I do not feel as though I can be wholly accepted there. Even though America portrays itself as a land of diversity, discrimination is prevalent. The September 11 tragedy is merely encouraging more of this. I am disappointed that you present yourselves as the most morally supreme people in the world, when in fact your government is equally irrational and corrupt. This unfairness has caused your downfall in foreign relations.

When you hurt or attempt to destroy the weak in the world, it is frequently and easily hushed and forgotten.

When you hurt or attempt to destroy the weak in the world, it is frequently and easily hushed and forgotten. The casualties are never a big deal simply because they cannot afford to plead mercy from the world through propaganda and the media as America often does. Your barbaric behavior in My Lai, Vietnam, is evidence of the masked nature of Americans. In the Middle

East you are careless in your impassive slaughter of very poor civilians, who for you become one with the enemy just because they share the same skin colour. Being a superpower, you comfortably play God, yet in doing so you perform the most atrocious of actions with the most evil of intentions. You work outside of the U.N. Why abuse it if the aim is to maintain world peace? Your enemies are immediately your associates one day for your financial or political benefits, and then bleeding foes the next when you backstab them as soon as you have used them. Now that time has back-fired on you. You expect the world to sympathize and form armies at your feet! The puppet governments you support are the sources of creation of enemies. That includes the series of political events in the Middle East, to the world's most wanted man, bin Laden. The September 11 tragedy would never have occurred and the War on Terror would not be playtime for Bush to use expensive arms and machines and station troops in regions where once again, America intends to dominate. The peacemaking and world-aid organizations you set up will not at all alleviate problems unless you change your foreign policies first.

I pray for the people on all war fronts that they may realize only good combats evil. Remove your veil of arrogance and selfish pride, and then perhaps you can truly combat the evils you are facing.

An adviser,

Vanessa Ferrolino

AUSTRALIA
SOUTH PACIFIC

Fiji

Australia

New Zealand

M. Brecke

SOLOMON ISLANDS

FANUATU

FIJI

NEW CALEDONIA

STRALIA

Fiji

WHERE	Oceania, island group in the South Pacific Ocean, about two-thirds of the way from Hawaii to New Zealand
SIZE	18,270 sq km, slightly smaller than New Jersey
POPULATION	880,874 (July 2004 est.)
INFANT MORTALITY	12.99 deaths/1,000 live births
THE PEOPLE	Fijian 51% (predominantly Melanesian with a Polynesian admixture), Indian 44%, European, other Pacific Islanders, overseas Chinese, and other 5%
RELIGIONS	Christian 52% (Methodist 37%, Roman Catholic 9%), Hindu 38%, Muslim 8%, other 2% *Note:* Fijians are mainly Christian, Indians are Hindu, and there is a Muslim minority
LANGUAGES	English (official), Fijian, Hindustani
LITERACY RATE	Total population: 93.7% male: 95.5% female: 91.9% (2003 est.)
GOVERNMENT	Republic
CAPITAL	Suva

FRANK ROCKY

FIJI

35 YEARS OLD, MALE, FARMER AND SCUBA INSTRUCTOR

Dear People of America,

When I was a little kid, I always thought I want to visit your country some day. I learn about it in school. I see the Golden Bridge in the movies, and I think, "Wow ... just look at that!" America looks so beautiful to me! But some of these movies make me feel scared too. They show me that America has more trouble, more violence than in Fiji. I guess America's got everything.

My country, Fiji, is really small—tiny. America is so big. We Fijians are all the same; you hardly see people from all over the world living in Fiji. But your America is for everyone. You accept every kind of people. You are so nice to welcome people from all over the world.

But the question is, why do people all over the world love to come to America? Because they have heard of it! Everyone learns about America. But people don't know about Fiji. When I visited America, I came across people who didn't even know where Fiji is! They never heard of it! They didn't even know that so many Fijians do live here in America right with them. It makes me feel how much I come from this little place. But I don't mind, it doesn't make me feel bad. Because

But if you learn to have patience, then maybe you can have this paradise in America, too.

M. Brecke

these Americans seemed excited to see me, to meet this little Fijian here in your big country.

The youth in Fiji are becoming Westernized, and I see that Fiji is changing really fast. When you go into town now, you see all the young people dressed differently—like women wearing shorts and tights. Before we didn't see that. But the parents still keep on with the traditional clothes. They wear a nice sulu. I think that's all O.K. Change is natural. It's fun. We also see new Western-style shops and businesses in Savusavu town, selling latte and pizza. I think if McDonald's will come to Savusavu, these youngsters will be very happy. They will like that a lot. It will be packed. Maybe the old people will say "Oh, here comes more America," but the young people are gonna love it.

I think the changes are O.K. because it's only in town, not in the traditional Fijian village. When the youngsters go back home to the village, they will be respectful to our culture. They will wear a sulu. They will be natural, like the little kids running around naked, and the women washing clothes in the river. The village is really tight. There are clans in the village, and if you don't respect tradition they will kick you out. People can't afford to live in town, and anyway they love the village, so the village will always be O.K. Only the towns might become more like America.

Maybe we Fijians could teach you Americans some things. Maybe we can teach you about patience. I know that your country has the control. I know America is strong. But you Americans have always to be in the hustle and the bustle. When you come to Fiji, you fall in love with our Fijian paradise. You relax in my home. You tell me you never want to leave. But if you learn to have patience, then maybe you can have this paradise in America, too.

In Fiji we have a phrase: "Maka leka." It means relax, no worries, have patience.

In Fiji we have a phrase: "*Maka leka*." It means relax, no worries, have patience. Everyone knows *maka leka* in Fiji, but can you Americans understand this? We have another expression known as "Fiji Time," which means, just take it easy, no hurry, don't rush. If you aim for three o'clock, maybe you get there at four. Maka leka. No problem. But we can afford to live that way in villages because many people in Fiji are not well educated. We just plant our crops, cassava and taro, and maybe fish a little. We can be on Fiji time. But then, we don't build a golden bridge. Our older people especially don't care about getting more money or changing things in the village. They like things the way they've always been. But they sure do like it when you Americans come to the village and give money to build a church or buy schoolbooks for the kids. We all know that Americans have the money.

What's amazing to me is how you Americans don't know your own neighbors. When I visited America, I saw people living in houses with all the doors and windows closed and you don't even know who lives next door. It's amazing! Sometimes you people come to Fiji and you meet other Americans who come from your same city back in the States. And you never did meet before! But in Fiji, everyone knows everyone. If you go in Fijian villages all the houses are just open. Everyone shares. They help one another. If one person needs to build a house, he will just say, "Hey, come on and help me build this house!" and other people in the village will help him build that house. Maybe he will mix kava for them, or make food. You never feel lonely in a Fijian village. But I think I might be lonely living in America, inside four walls with all the doors and windows shut. You should get to know your neighbors. That's how you guys are gonna help each other.

You should get to know your neighbors. That's how you guys are gonna help each other.

Last, I have to tell you that I think American women are awesome. They're sexy and beautiful. They take good care of me. In Fiji, when you go around with someone in the village, everyone knows, and it's important which family goes together. But when I am with an American woman it's more open. We hold hands, and walk in the streets and can kiss. In a Fijian village it's different. We don't display affection like that. It's not good in front of the children. But I like the openness of the American women. And I love all the people that I get to know from America. Every single one. If I was to move to America, I would get to know each one of you and I would love you all.

Lolomas,

Frank Rocky

Australia

WHERE	Oceania, continent between the Indian Ocean and the South Pacific Ocean
SIZE	7,686,850 sq km, slightly smaller than the U.S. contiguous 48 states
POPULATION	19,913,144 (July 2004 est.)
INFANT MORTALITY	4.76 deaths/1,000 live births
THE PEOPLE	Caucasian 92%, Asian 7%, aboriginal and other 1%
RELIGIONS	Anglican 26.1%, Roman Catholic 26%, other Christian 24.3%, non-Christian 11%, other 12.6%
LANGUAGES	English, native languages
LITERACY RATE	Total population: 100%
GOVERNMENT	Democratic, federal-state system recognizing the British monarch as sovereign
CAPITAL	Canberra

LINDA J. WELLS

AUSTRALIA
40 YEARS OLD, FEMALE,
COMMUNITY DEVELOPMENT AND TRAINING OFFICER

Dear People of America,

How are you? I can't begin to imagine how it must be.
Who are you?

Mickey Mouse or Ronald Muckdonald or the CIA, George W, Julia Roberts, Alice Walker, a strident tourist, or a schoolboy who shot up all of his colleagues? These are the most salient images of America that reach me here in the centre of Australia.

Are you any one of those, some of these, or none of the above? Are you responsible for the inane nonsense that comes to us from yours, the biggest brother nation on earth, or are you, the folk, just trying to live amongst it, trying to hold your heads up high above the sewerage that threatens to drown us all?

I'll tell you a little story. When I was pregnant with my daughter, I told her, developing within me, "There's three things you won't be getting, kid, in the interests of wellbeing. That's food from Muckdonald's, Coca Cola, and Barbie dolls." Note the common links. They're all junk and they all come out of the "greatest" nation on earth, the United States of America.

By the age of nine, of course, she's had them all whether I wanted her

to or not. I mellowed on the Barbies, actually. I like the way she arranges them and acts out social dramas. It's a part of her healthy development. It's the blondness and the bustiness and the unrealistic skinniness of the Barbies I take offense to. And the price. It's hard when she needs a grandma for the game, or an old uncle, or a fat lady. Could you get Mattel to come up with a few members of Barbie's extended family to make the game complete? Various shapes and sizes and colours.

Anyway, it's hard to avoid that insidious, all pervasive, enterprise-driven junk without running away. And to where could one run? Where do you go to escape from the greatest imperialist nation on earth and all of its dodgy exports?

I won one round. As a toddler, my daughter would ask for Muckdonald's. "Mummy, can we have Muckdonald's? Can we have Muckdonalds? Can we have Muckdonald's?" Nag, nag, nag. Tough mummy says, "No, it's not good for you, it's rubbish. It will make you sick." She seemed to quietly accept that, took it on board. Good little girl. One day we were driving past the Muckdonald's store in our town—golden arches, drive-through section, convenient car park, the works. As we drove past the whole arrangement, an ambulance was driving out of the car park. "Look mummy," my little girl exclaimed, "an ambulance. Someone ate too much Muckdonald's!"

Where do you go to escape from the greatest imperialist nation on earth and all of its dodgy exports?

Muckdonald's food is full of fat and sugar and salt. Thanks for that. Clever advertising and no advice to the contrary misleads people into thinking it's a viable nutritional option. So they eat up big. And they get heart disease. And they get diabetes. And they get high blood pressure. And Ronald Muckdonald and the Colonel and The Real Thing and all their mates laugh all the way to the bank, while people in my town get sick and die.

That fast food should come with warnings, just like cigarettes do these days:

TOO MANY FRIES WILL MAKE YOU DIE

TOO MUCH PATTY WILL MAKE YOU FATTY

WARNING: THE COLONEL'S SECRET RECIPE IS A HEALTH HAZARD

But the Statue of Liberty wouldn't like that, would she? Freedom. Isn't that your driving force? But, "Freedom's just another word for nothing left to lose." Thanks, Janis.

Did I mention Pine Gap? It's nestled in the rocky red hills, just twenty kilometres from our town. You don't see it much, unless you're looking. It's a whole lot of shiny white domes that stand out amongst the ancient rockery of the desert landscape, well defined in an almost impenetrable fence and patrolled by soldiers of the American military, just in case. An American military spy base. What fun! The U.S.A. pays a peppercorn in rent once in every ten years, or so the story goes. Why should you pay to keep something here that is so very good for our nation? Our security? Our protection? If the "enemy" manages to cross the lines and destroy the base, we here, in this little town in the middle of the desert, go first. It is this that hangs over the

So they eat up big.
And they get heart disease.
And they get diabetes.
And they get high blood pressure.

heads of the people of Alice Springs. Those of us who don't trust American foreign policy.

I don't like the way Australia, as a nation, looks up to America, as a nation. I don't take responsibility for that, which is why I'm reluctant to blame you, the people of America, for the follies of your country. No matter how loudly I speak to the leaders of my country, it falls on deaf ears. Do you know what I mean? Probably, because your leaders seem to be my leaders' big brothers and they say, "You wanna fight the filthy commies in Vietnam? No worries, we'll conscript our men."

I don't like the way Australia, as a nation, looks up to America, as a nation.

"You wanna bomb Afghanistan to pieces in the vain hope that we get enemy number one, no matter how many innocents fall by the wayside in the process? No worries, we'll stand beside you."

"You wanna lead an attack on Iraq for amassing weapons of mass destruction, this attack being against the better judgement of the U.N. and the European nations? No worries Big Brother George, we'll be there."

"Wherever you want to go and whoever you want to attack, for whatever reason, Big Brother, we'll stand there, beside you or behind you or in front of you. Haven't we always followed you and done what you wanted us to do? And we love you, Big Brother. And you must always be right."

What does your culture do besides consume, be silent, die? Your movie stars seem to get paid more money than anyone else. Why? Because they have tight arses and come-on smiles? Because through their work they can help folk to escape from the reality that is their lives?

Don't get me wrong, I've met some fantastic Americans— considerate, compassionate, articulate, dynamic, generous people. When yanks take that cultural confidence and individuality and put it to good purpose, the results are truly inspiring.

I think we all have to rise above the ignorance. We have to be honest about what we value and what we need and what it is that really matters and live accordingly.

I think we all have to rise above the ignorance. We have to be honest about what we value and what we need and what it is that really matters and live accordingly.

Dear people of America, I'll be seeing you.

Love from Linda

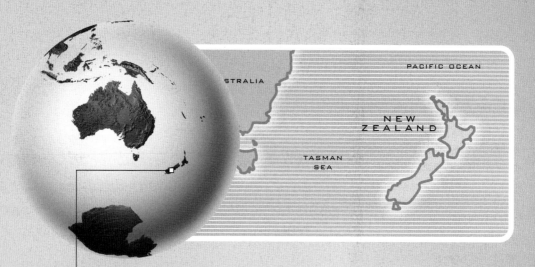

NEW ZEALAND

WHERE	Oceania, islands in the South Pacific Ocean, southeast of Australia
SIZE	268,680 sq km, about the size of Colorado
POPULATION	3,993,817 (July 2004 est.)
INFANT MORTALITY	5.96 deaths/1,000 live births
THE PEOPLE	New Zealand European 74.5%, Maori 9.7%, other European 4.6%, Pacific Islander 3.8%, Asian and others 7.4%
RELIGIONS	Anglican 24%, Presbyterian 18%, Roman Catholic 15%, Methodist 5%, Baptist 2%, other Protestant 3%, unspecified or none 33%
LANGUAGES	English (official), Maori (official)
LITERACY RATE	Total population: 99%
GOVERNMENT	Parliamentary democracy
CAPITAL	Wellington

DEBORAH RHODE

NEW ZEALAND

55 YEARS OLD, FEMALE, TEACHER AND GRADUATE STUDENT

Dear People of America,

In New Zealand we call it the Tall Poppy Syndrome. The Tall Poppy is one who stands out—is more successful than those around it—a person, a group, a team who achieves greatness. Unlike America, where success and fame (for whatever reason), is admired and idolised, it has become an Australasian characteristic to "knock down the Tall Poppy" as they don't fit into our traditional egalitarian ethic. After the initial adulation, successful people are targets for criticism in the public domain. They become victims of the Tall Poppy Syndrome. While we all know this is a New Zealand trait, we're not really proud of it—no one will admit to being a perpetrator.

Kiwis are known for their friendliness and hospitality—when you come here as independent visitors you will be welcomed openheartedly. You are known for your openness, worldliness, and success. But once we start to talk of international politics, economics, religion, or corporatization—Americans, you're in trouble for being a Tall Poppy!

I have tried to understand why "Americans" seem to get blamed for everything. Having lived in Colorado for a few years (and having been married to an American), I've known you individually, have wonderful

memories of visiting your country, experienced great hospitality, and have treasured friendships. My first recollection of American friendliness was when I arrived in Denver as a twenty-two–year old, it seemed everyone on the street smiled and said Hi! I hadn't even met these people and they were so openly friendly. Having been raised in Britain, I couldn't get over this! And in restaurants, waiters were sometimes overwhelmingly gregarious (though I later realised this was strongly motivated by the tipping system). In New Zealand we don't tip–staff are all paid a standard wage. There's an upside and a downside to this: waiters here are only friendly when they feel like it, but when they are friendly they really mean it!

So why do you get blamed for everything? You are both admired and envied, your confidence sometimes seems like arrogance, you polarise people's opinions and challenge their prejudices. You're too much, too big, too powerful, too influential, too successful … too global. And this I think is the problem: capitalism, internationalism, globalisation, or "the West" has become synonymous with "American."

And this I think is the problem: capitalism, internationalism, globalisation or "the West" has become synonymous with "American."

We love to be hypocrites. We complain Americans are buying up our houses and lands and inflating prices (though I don't hear complaints from the sellers); when we buy land in the Pacific Islands, we are "helping their economy." We complain about American tourists inflating prices for locals, forgetting that there would often be no local economy without tourism. We complain about American junk food, and eat it with relish.

America, you're a Tall Poppy. You are successful. You stand out in the field as being taller, bigger, better. While we know we can't be like you, your success gives you power that makes us feel small. We feel uncomfortable that your power can overwhelm other small countries like us.

When you come to New Zealand you may be blamed for all the ills of the globalised world. But it's not you Americans—don't take it personally! But Corporate America threatens us. We have always had an easy-going attitude towards life and we don't really want business life to become hectic, impersonal, cut-throat, and competitive. But we can see that this behaviour may become necessary to compete in the global business environment. And as for politics … Yes, you are big and powerful and with politicians who behave like politicians instead of human beings. I don't agree with your foreign policy, I abhor your government's recent mobilisation in Iraq, and years of covert intervention in the governments of others.

But we're all people of the world, individuals who—even in democratic societies—generally have little control over (or under) our governments.

Wouldn't it be so much better if we could all get away from nationalistic labels—and just be us?

Deborah

AMERICAS

ARGENTINA

PERU

BRAZIL

GUATEMALA

HONDURAS

CANADA

M. Brecke

ARGENTINA

WHERE	Southern South America, bordering the South Atlantic Ocean, between Chile and Uruguay
SIZE	2,766,890 sq km, slightly less than three-tenths the size of the US
POPULATION	39,144,753 (July 2004 est.)
INFANT MORTALITY	15.6 deaths/1,000 live births
THE PEOPLE	White (mostly Spanish and Italian) 97%, Mestizo, Amerindian, or other nonwhite groups 3%
RELIGIONS	Nominally Roman Catholic 92% (less than 20% practicing), Protestant 2%, Jewish 2%, other 4%
LANGUAGES	Spanish (official), English, Italian, German, French
LITERACY RATE	Total population: 97.1% (2003 est.)
GOVERNMENT	Republic
CAPITAL	Buenos Aires

VIRGINIA DI PAOLO

ARGENTINA

20 YEARS OLD, FEMALE, DANCER

Dear People of America,

I've learned something from you that will never be touched upon in my country of Argentina. I've never been to America, but I had the great experience to meet an American man who I have developed a very nice friendship with. As our relationship was growing up, our interest and curiosity in each other's cultures and countries was growing as well. My friend is a well-traveled man. He told me about beautiful cities around the world where he has been. He has a way of describing people, places, and situations that made it easy for me to imagine all of them. His voice was always full of excitement and joy. But it was especially so when he was speaking about his own country. About America, he would be speaking with his heart. I could feel that.

When it was my turn to tell about my place, I felt moved and ashamed by the fact that I couldn't speak with so much pride about it. I didn't love my country. I didn't know how.

We Argentinians are always too focused on the negatives issues. That stress on the negative make us forget all the gifts that we have been given and all the battles that we've gone through to become a democratic and free nation. So, in my need to show my friend the good side of Argentina, I started

M. Brecke

to look inside. And as I was looking for beauty I began to see it more and more. And much to my surprise, I realized that I have many things to be proud of. I slowly started to feel what I felt in my friend's voice—love for my country. And that new feeling was truly amazing.

And that is how I finally comprehend why there are so many of my people who seem to dislike America. It is because we Argentinians do not love our own country. Thus we cannot love others. I know that we all would like to be like America. You have the best blessing: your people love you whatever happens.

Whether you believe me or not let me tell you: it doesn't happen like this everywhere. At least it doesn't here in Argentina. So now I want you to know that I feel extraordinarily grateful to have been given such a teaching in my life.

Thank you America!

Sincerely,

Virgy

p.s. I could have written to you about what most Argentinians think of America, but I wouldn't be authentic. I want to speak for me, not for others. I have my heart totally open. But most Argentinians have their hearts closed, and their minds are narrow. If they open their hearts, their minds will follow (*es muy simple!*).

Besides, every country has flaws (en mayor o menor medida). No country is immune to them.

But you may want to know that a great percent of the Argentine population have their hearts full of rancor. They still cannot forget the fact that the U.S. supported and financed all the non-communist dictatorships around the world, including the military dictatorship that my country suffered from 1976 to 1983. This is but one of the many old rancors.

These days, most people in Argentina can't stand the way that we are being subjugated by your government. The U.S. lends us a lot of money but the ways of paying are very difficult. Taxes are raised day after day. The interests are too high.

What I do think is a crime is how your government acts with such poor countries like Uganda or any other country from Black Africa. I cannot understand why America cannot forgive the little amount of money that those countries owe to you in order to allow them to have a better kind of life. I don't think you could be affected by those debts. Those countries cannot produce money or food or medicines—nothing. Their poor die in the poorest way. As I see it, it is like if you had one million dollars and I had only one dollar to live. But because I owe you money, you would force me to pay you back, letting me die, instead of letting me live. I don't want to sound aggressive, but it's like your country behaves like a usurer sometimes.

But I don't want to get into a political issue, because I am too young to judge what is wrong or right with America. That's even hard for my own behavior!

Besides, every country has flaws (*en mayor o menor medida*). No country is immune to them. Please just know that I love your country with all my heart as it is tacitly said in my letter.

PERU

WHERE	Western South America, bordering the South Pacific Ocean, between Chile and Ecuador
SIZE	1,285,220 sq km, slightly smaller than Alaska
POPULATION	27,544,305 (July 2004 est.)
INFANT MORTALITY	32.95 deaths/1,000 live births
THE PEOPLE	Amerindian 45%, mestizo (mixed Amerindian and white) 37%, white 15%, black, Japanese, Chinese, and other 3%
RELIGIONS	Roman Catholic 90%
LANGUAGES	Spanish (official), Quechua (official), Aymara
LITERACY RATE	Total population: 90.9% male: 95.2% female: 86.8% (2003 est.)
GOVERNMENT	Constitutional republic
CAPITAL	Lima

JUAN CARLOS MACHICADO

PERU

39 YEARS OLD, MALE, TOUR GUIDE

Dear People of America,

The truth of what you hear everywhere is relative. Governments lie a lot to their citizens in order to keep power. Your country is no exception to this rule. What's worse is that your politicians make you see politics as something boring and difficult to understand. They make you numb. All you know is that you have to go to the supermarkets, buy food, fill your stomachs, and watch your big screen televisions. The majority of you don't participate in the real destiny of your country.

You don't question your government as to why you have cheap products in stores like Walmart and Target. You don't question, because you can't face the truth: a lot of people in countries like mine are being badly paid and exploited for their labor so that you can have what you want. You ignore that military Latin American forces are trained by you in a military academy called "the School of the Americas" in your very own Fort Bening, Georgia. They are trained to kill union leaders and workers, people just like you, in Latin countries every time they make demonstrations on the streets for better salaries and living conditions.

I, for one, don't want to live like you do. We Latin people have a tremendous cultural richness and background of our own. Just imagine a world where everybody would have to eat only in McDonalds, Burger Kings, or in non-tasty Taco Bells. What if the whole planet was covered with your strip malls? Wouldn't you get bored of life on Earth?

If there is to remain a variety of cultures on our planet, it will be because we come to learn a lot from each other and benefit all together instead of killing each other. We now have a lot of people dying of starvation, malnutrition, and violence simply because of the economic rules of the International Monetary Fund (IMF), and other similar institutions. These are helped by your government to apply economic punishments if we don't play on your terms.

All doctrines and philosophies on our planet teach us, "Love for each other." It is time to pay attention to this spiritual teaching, otherwise we will destroy ourselves and our planet.

I do love the American people, and I have a lot of wonderful friends in your country. I just don't like the politics of your government. They sell you stupid ideas like being the "superpower" and "God Bless America." God is all over the world, blessing all life. And if you think you are so intelligent, then you should share your "superpower wisdom" to make of this entire planet, not your home only, a Paradise.

We all need to participate actively in the creation of our future. The problems that we face today are not only local problems anymore. We all share the same problems and we depend on the good will of each other. The only way we will survive is by growing spiritually. By saying that I mean treating each other with love and understanding. We need to educate ourselves to avoid the manipulations of those few whose only motivation is to benefit from our labor. All doctrines and philosophies on our planet teach us, "Love for each other." It is time to pay attention to this spiritual teaching, otherwise we will destroy ourselves and our planet.

Let me finish by sharing with you an Inka teaching and thinking: "We came to this planet to take care of the creation of the creator, and we were given a special brain to live in harmony with all the elements of nature." Our planet is alive, rich, and wonderful. Let's keep it that way!

In order to keep harmony, my ancestors didn't have in their native language the word "friend." They all treated each other with respect as brother and sister:

A man to another man calls *waykey* (brother).

A man to a woman calls *panay* (sister).

A woman to another woman calls *ñañay* (sister).

A woman to a man calls *turay* (brother).

Your *waykey* always,

Juan Carlos Machicado

"We came to this planet to take care of the creation of the creator, and we were given a special brain to live in harmony with all the elements of nature."

Brazil

WHERE	Eastern South America, bordering the Atlantic Ocean
SIZE	8,511,965 sq km, slightly smaller than the U.S.
POPULATION	184,101,109
INFANT MORTALITY	30.66 deaths/1,000 live births
THE PEOPLE	White (includes Portuguese, German, Italian, Spanish, Polish) 55%, mixed white and black 38%, black 6%, other (includes Japanese, Arab, Amerindian) 1%
RELIGIONS	Roman Catholic (nominal) 80%
LANGUAGES	Portuguese (official), Spanish, English, French
LITERACY RATE	Total population: 86.4% male: 86.1% female: 86.6% (2003 est.)
GOVERNMENT	Federative republic
CAPITAL	Brasilia

MARINA PEIXOTO

BRAZIL

26 YEARS OLD, FEMALE, INDUSTRIAL ENGINEER

Dear People of America,

Your culture has always influenced my life and I think my whole generation. As a child it all started with Disney characters and that world of dreams. Then when I was a teenager American music was played in every party I used to go to. Madonna was an icon. After the success of McDonalds hamburgers, many other stores tried to adopt an English name to attract people, because at that time being American was cool. Parents started giving American names to their children as a symbol of status, people used American flags on their clothes, a mall was built with a copy of the Liberty statue in the front door. At the same time, many people started criticizing this positioning, saying that we should valorize our own culture instead. My parents used to say that this was the way-of-life of what we call "new rich people." These are the people who don't belong to any of the traditional families, but won a lot of money recently and love to imitate Americans. And they were somehow right, because Barra da Tijuca, one neighborhood in Rio, was created in American image. It's mainly like Miami, with all those highways and buildings, and it's now the main residence of these "new riches."

After the globalization process I was happy to have access to American products that used to be too expensive before. But then after Bush started the war with Iraq I saw that Brazilian people started to be ashamed of having American symbols. Some threw tomatoes on the mall, some restaurants stopped selling American products and so on. A new feeling against the American imperialism was born in my heart and the hearts

of Brazilian people. I started to realize that all those years we were submitting to your power and we lost a lot of our identity and culture. However, I still believe that we can continue to share knowledge, values, and culture—and we could all win with this exchange if it was made in a fair way.

I'm working for an American company, so business is also impacting my life. Additionally, I have finished an exchange program for an MBA at the University of Illinois, where I've lived for five months and could learn more about your culture and your way of life. I had many opportunities that I wouldn't have in Brazil. For instance, during these five months, I had four different jobs and you accepted me even without having experience and being a foreigner. So I changed my mind about what I thought, that you were a little bit arrogant and that you didn't really like us. I also worked at the stadium during football games and I've learned some interesting things, such as that you like Coke with a lot of ice, which is not common in Brazil. If I tried to sell like this here, people would say that I was trying to rob them, since part of the volume on the cup would be water from the ice and they were paying for Coke. I also found interesting the way you make every game become a spectacle, with all the cheerleaders and a band. The food was somehow disappointing for me, since it wasn't as healthy as I used to eat at home. I ate a lot of hamburgers and hot dogs instead of real meals, and fruits were extremely expensive.

The obedience to law, together with your freedom of expression, made me feel I was really in the country of liberty and opportunities.

I observed your culture and was happily surprised with the respect to customer's rights that you have. The obedience to law, together with your freedom of expression, made me feel I was really in the country of liberty and opportunities. It was amazing how people really ask your identity to buy alcohol drinks and everybody respects the rules of not drinking in the street and not making noise late at night. Whenever something strange happened on the streets, the policeman quickly arrived and everything was extremely organized and worked with effectiveness. I made a lot of friends, experienced the Thanksgiving ritual with an American family and had unforgettable moments.

I would have said that it was perfect if I didn't have some disappointments with you. During the MBA classes, I could feel your prejudice against people from other countries and a lack of knowledge of what exists in the rest of the world. You are very competitive and individualist and I could only get respect after I took good grades and could show you that you are not

We could improve your culture as well as yours improving ours.

the only good ones. I was also surprised with some questions you asked me, so I would like to clarify some doubts you might still have. First of all, Buenos Aires is not the capital of Brazil; it belongs to Argentina. Although both countries are in South America, we speak Portuguese and they speak Spanish. I live in Rio de Janeiro, which is a big city, not a jungle. We have buildings, cars, malls, and ordinary people don't get naked during Carnival.

Anyway, as much as I could learn with you during this five months, I would be happy if you could learn a little bit more about not only Brazil, but about all the rest of the world, our food, our dances, music, habits, flexibility and creativity to solve problems, and about environmental respect. We could improve your culture as well as yours improving ours. Maybe it would be a good idea to change your educational system, so that the American children can start learning about others from the beginning. If you are more aware of what happens around the world and learn more about us, maybe you could be more diplomatic and democratic to solve problems without a war.

Marina Peixoto

If you are more aware of what happens around the world and learn more about us, maybe you could be more diplomatic and democratic to solve problems without a war.

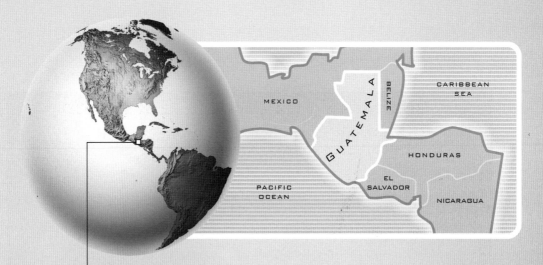

GUATEMALA

WHERE	Middle America, bordering the Caribbean Sea, between Honduras and Belize and bordering the North Pacific Ocean, between El Salvador and Mexico
SIZE	108,890 sq km, slightly smaller than Tennessee
POPULATION	14,280,596 (July 2004 est.)
INFANT MORTALITY	36.91 deaths/1,000 live births
THE PEOPLE	Mestizo (mixed Amerindian-Spanish or assimilated Amerindian—in local Spanish called Ladino), approximately 55%, Amerindian or predominantly Amerindian, approximately 43%, whites and others 2%
RELIGIONS	Roman Catholic, Protestant, indigenous Mayan beliefs
LANGUAGES	Spanish 60%, Amerindian languages 40% (23 officially recognized Amerindian languages, including Quiche, Cakchiquel, Kekchi, Mam, Garifuna, and Xinca)
LITERACY RATE	Total population: 70.6% male: 78% female: 63.3% (2003 est.)
GOVERNMENT	Constitutional democratic republic
CAPITAL	Guatemala City

CLARISSA LUZ GARCIA GONZALES

GUATEMALA

14 YEARS OLD, FEMALE, STUDENT

Dear People of America,

I would like to start by saying that I just wrote, "Dear People of America" instead of "Dear People of the United States" because that as how we were told to start the letter. I'm not okay with you people calling yourselves Americans, because I'm also American and I'm not from the U.S.A. An American can be anyone from the continents of North, Central, and South America.

I am really sorry for what happened on September 11. There's no excuse for what those awful people did. They have been punished or shall be punished in their due time by God. Another thing I'm really sorry about is all the innocent people that are dying in Afghanistan due to the attack you are doing there. I don't know the exact number of innocent people who have died in Afghanistan, but I can assure you that it's more than the people who died in September 11. What this tells me is that you think that the killing of people in the U.S. is wrong but the killing of Afghans is okay. If your country is truly Christian and you believe in God you should stop those killings, because killing is against God's rules. Right now bombing Afghanistan is not giving you a good reputation; its actually giving you the reputation of terrorists, the ones you are trying to fight. And this reputation is the one that told the terrorist from September 11 to do what they did, because they think you are the bad guys. This reputation is the one you gained when you dropped the atomic bomb in Japan and did a lot of other terrible things. When we look at your country we look at a rich and powerful country that has helped many countries, but we also see a country that has done terrible things.

I admire how schools work and how they are available to everyone in the United States, but it doesn't work that way here in Latin American countries and in many other parts of the world. The public schools are bad, and not even half of the population has education. That's why I think communism would bring a positive aspect to our lives. In Cuba, everyone gets good, free education, and they all have something to eat. I don't think the embargo in Cuba is very fair because some Cubans love Fidel Castro and his way of governing and you should let them be free. If Cubans don't like Fidel Castro they'll eventually be heard and he will be kicked out. Of course, there are some people that don't like Fidel Castro, just like there are some people that don't like George W. Bush. You say people suffer there and want to get out of the country and that's why they run away to the United States. Well, in many Latin American countries people suffer, they don't have money to buy food for their children, and that's

When we look at your country we look at a rich and powerful country that has helped many countries, but we also see a country that has done terrible things.

why they too go to the U.S. in search of a better life. I think the embargo is stopping Cuba from progressing and having a better economy and everything, and you should give them a chance to see if things work out for them with a communist government.

You are a rich, powerful country. Use your money and influences wisely.

I also think bombing Iraq was wrong. I know many Americans didn't want this war to happen, but many felt very proud and eager to go fight and kill men, women, and children in the name of democracy and their country. Again, sometimes its good that you help a country out of a problem, but sometimes it's just better to leave them alone or just give them a little bit of help. I don't think killing all those people was the solution to their problem. If you were looking for one man, Hussein, you could have done better than just dropping bombs on all the innocent people.

You are a rich, powerful country. Use your money and influences wisely.

Thank you,

Clarissa

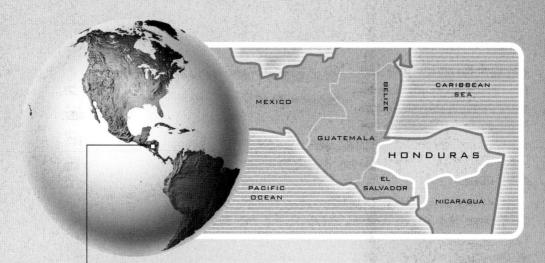

Honduras

WHERE	Middle America, bordering the Caribbean Sea, between Guatemala and Nicaragua and bordering the North Pacific Ocean, between El Salvador and Nicaragua
SIZE	112,090 sq km, slightly larger than Tennessee
POPULATION	6,823,568 *Note*: estimates for this country explicitly take into account the effects of excess mortality due to AIDS
INFANT MORTALITY	29.64 deaths/1,000 live births
THE PEOPLE	Mestizo (mixed Amerindian and European) 90%, Amerindian 7%, black 2%, white 1%
RELIGIONS	Roman Catholic 97%, Protestant minority
LANGUAGES	Spanish, Amerindian dialects
LITERACY RATE	Total population: 76.2% male: 76.1% female: 76.3% (2003 est.)
GOVERNMENT	Democratic constitutional republic
CAPITAL	Tegucigalpa

238

MARIA FERNANDA AVILA

HONDURAS

13 YEARS OLD, FEMALE, STUDENT

Dear People of America,

Thanks for giving me this chance to express myself. My name is María Fernanda Avila, I am thirteen years old, and I study at a bilingual school here in Honduras. Everybody knows that Latin America has a huge problem of immigration because our countries are very poor. We, the people of Latin America, have a lot of moral and spiritual values and when we believe in something it is very hard to make us change our minds. Many of us don't have enough money to have all the things necessary for a good living.

Many Latin American people would make such a long and dangerous journey to the U.S.A. with one idea on their minds, and that idea is hope. They have the hope that when they get there, all the pain and suffering would be worth it—and also a whole new world of opportunities would be open so they can start all over again. These types of experiences happen in my country almost every day, and when they appear on the news I imagine the great fear and struggle that they feel. Not only the people that left, also the people that are left behind hoping that their family, friends, etc. will make it safely to the U.S.A.

After reaching that goal of having a job and earning enough money, all of them can dream of coming back home. I don't blame them wishing to come home. It doesn't matter how big and industrialized the United States is, it is not a better place than home.

I remember that when I was in the United States, I couldn't wake up without feeling the intense heat or seeing a twenty-four–hour cement landscape, and when I'm in Honduras I can wake up every morning with a cool breeze and seeing trees everywhere. We are a small country, but I'm proud of being what I am. I am proud to call myself a "catracha." We could learn a lot of things from you like your economy and tourism, but if you ask me you could learn from us, because just being so powerful wouldn't mean that you are perfect, because sometimes you are so artificial that you don't have time to see the beauty of nature.

We both can learn from each other. I think the governments in the world could stop trying to always say they are right, instead of doing what's right. They could stop using peace as an excuse to keep fighting, then nobody would have to suffer the effects of war. What if wars weren't even held on Earth? We humans have God's gift of intelligence and we should use it to reason to each other, to talk the problems in a specific way, but instead we use it to create weapons to destroy. We all live on this wonderful planet, and we all share the same things. Why should people fight if at the end we are all the same and have the same needs?

Instead of using money on creating weapons or taking revenge, we should use money to help the poor countries and the people that inhabit them. We should offer this help without hoping anything in exchange. We should not help only during disasters or to look good, but always. I think that way, all of us can live happily and with better opportunities in life—in our very own land, without looking for happiness in other places.

We should offer this help without hoping anything in exchange. We should not help only during disasters or to look good, but always.

Sincerely,

Maria Fernanda Avila

CANADA

WHERE	Northern North America, bordering the North Atlantic Ocean on the east, North Pacific Ocean on the west, and the Arctic Ocean on the north, north of the conterminous U.S.
SIZE	9,976,140 sq km, somewhat larger than the U.S.
POPULATION	32,507,874 (July 2004 est.)
INFANT MORTALITY	4.82 deaths/1,000 live births
THE PEOPLE	British Isles origin 28%, French origin 23%, other European 15%, Amerindian 2%, other, mostly Asian, African, Arab 6%, mixed background 26%
RELIGIONS	Roman Catholic 46%, Protestant 36%, other 18% *Note*: based on the 1991 census
LANGUAGES	English 59.3% (official), French 23.2% (official), other 17.5%
LITERACY RATE	Total population: 97%
GOVERNMENT	Confederation with parliamentary democracy
CAPITAL	Ottawa

Austin Repath

Canada

67 years old, male, writer

Dear People of America,

Many times I have traveled across your country, been delighted by your warm and friendly manner, and enchanted by the beauty of your land. Since my youth, I have marveled at your glorious break from Old World traditions, the free-spirited way you live, and how you established a constitution that enshrined freedom and democracy. You have created a culture like no other since the ancient Greeks.

At the same time, I sense that you are struggling with what you should be about. May I, a good neighbor to your north, offer a few observations?

Being a Canadian, I have watched and studied you with both a critical and an admiring eye, in the same manner a younger brother might a successful older brother. I marvel at your willingness to experiment and try new things. You have an energy and an unabashed enthusiasm for everything you enter into, whether it be to win Olympic gold medals, put a man on the moon, or simply get out there and live life to the fullest. I love this about you.

I grew up believing in the wisdom, the common sense, and goodness of the American people. I remember an earlier America where people accepted another's word, sealed a contract with a handshake, spoke what

they thought. However, this way of being in the world appears to have all but died within your people. I hope and pray that it will return.

For I have watched as you have changed into something that makes me uncomfortable. To begin with, I find frightening the hold that unquestioned religious belief has on many people in your country; frightening because in my opinion their beliefs haven't matured. They seem to spend more of their time trying to force their moral code on others, rather than using what they believe to transform themselves.

Also, many of you are given to seeing Americans as larger and more special than the rest of humanity. A little awareness that we all share a frail and fragile existence would, to say the least, be helpful to all concerned. At the same time the fact remains that you are a people who have wealth and influence. You believe that you have much to offer the world. You, the people of America, perhaps by birth, by place, by accident, or by fate, have been chosen to lead the world. You sense this.

I remember an earlier America where people accepted another's word, sealed a contract with a handshake, spoke what they thought.

These days, you have chosen to lead the world in the fight against terrorism. I fully realize the need, and I support your fight. At the same time (I care about you too much not to say this) I think you have lost your way, may even have forgotten your destiny.

In this regard, may I offer a few suggestions. Begin at home. Care for those who are kin. I cannot help but sense that you are deeply troubled by the pain you see on your sidewalks. Rescuing the homeless from your streets, saving the addicted from themselves, taking guns away from your young people, it seems to me, should take priority.

Your nation has a unique tradition of helping. You have been extremely generous to nations who have suffered war and famine. Can you not turn this generosity toward your own tired and poor? You need only awaken to what is asleep within you, what you have enshrined in your Statute of Liberty, and what perhaps defines you more than you know—your great generosity. By caring for those among you who cannot help themselves sends a message that you are a compassionate people.

You are, in my opinion, a nation desperate for a task worthy of who you are.

Personally, I see you as a people longing for a task that would call forth the best in you, a challenge that would bring out your greatness. You are, in my opinion, a nation desperate for a task worthy of who you are. The redistribution of wealth, developing a new energy source, eliminating poverty, pioneering a new world on Mars—these would be endeavors that would stir the soul, test your mettle, and make you worthy of all that you have been blessed with.

Such undertakings call forth sacrifice and commitment that bring out a nobility of spirit and transform a nation. Historically, they leave behind a legacy worthy of a great people. In undertaking such a noble endeavor you lead the world by doing what others cannot.

Finally, I would that you never forget the compassion and vision that has made you the people you are.

Austin Repath

Some Questions for Discussion

1. Is it important for Americans to learn about how the U.S. impacts and has impacted other nations of the world? Why or Why Not?

2. Why is it important to know about how other countries view the U.S.?

3. Why is it important that we are educated about the world's cultures and nations?

4. What does globalization mean and what are some of its effects?

5. What are some stereotypes that people have about Americans?

6. What are stereotypes that you have about people in other countries?

7. What does being an American mean to you?

8. How does American media influence other cultures? Give examples.

9. What do you want to tell citizens of the world about being an American?

10. Some other citizens of the world are of the opinion that money is synonymous with God in America. What does this mean? What do you think?

11. If you could travel to any other country in the world, which would it be? What do you think the people are like there? How are they the same or different than you?

12. How can you be more active in creating positive change on a global scale?

About the Author

Erica Geller was born in New York and has lived in the San Francisco Bay area since 1996. It is her love of creative expression and a desire to help promote peaceful coexistence that inspires her work with *Letters to America*.

About the photographer

Mark Brecke is a San Francisco-based independent international documentary photographer and filmmaker. His work has taken him to 40 countries, and he has photographed in some of the world's most troubled regions, including Cambodia, Rwanda, Sudan, Kosovo, the West Bank, and Iraq. His recent film, *War as a Second Language*, is currently screening in film festivals and galleries, and was selected for the 2004 Amnesty International Film Festival.

Acknowledgements

It took the contribution of many people to form this collection. I wish I could name you all. Thank you especially to approximately 600 of you who wrote to *Letters to America*. Thank you to the authors in this book for courageously sharing yourselves.

Maggie Holmes brilliantly burst the original thought that we later transformed into *Letters to America*. I thank her for her creativity, insight, hard work, support, love, and beauty. Without you, *Letters* would not be.

Thank you, Nick Randolph, for your incredible support. I am infinitely grateful for your unshakable belief in me and for helping bring LTA into being. Thank you for being a positive and powerful force in the world.

Many thanks to Steven Scholl, Gary Kliewer, Christy Collins and everyone at RiverWood Books.

Thank you, Mark Brecke, for the way you walk in the world, for the way you hold its image.

Thank you to our Website stars and dear friends: Kevin Merrit, Jason Seidler, and Rick Starbuck.

Thank you to my amazingly supportive family and tribe of superstar friends.

Thank you to the organizations and people that helped to bring Letters to America to fruition:

Kim and Muna McQuay, and the Asia Foundation–Bangladesh

Scott Snyder and Kimberly Lehn, and the Asia Foundation–South Korea

Elka Dacheva, Birgitta Cattelle, and Allen Stevens at The American College of Sofia–Bulgaria

Shelley Wowchuk at the Anglo American School–Bulgaria

Jan Zlatan Kulenovic and the Balkin Children and Youth Foundation

The Child Welfare League Foundation–Taiwan

Gregory T. Absten and The Cuban Health Network–Florida

Margo Squire, Lala Rzayeva, Fariz Ismailzade, and The Eurasia Foundation-Azerbaijan

Stephen Schmida and the Eurasia Foundation–Russia

Shafi Mohammad and Humanitarian Assistance for the Women and Children of Afghanistan (HAWCA)–Pakistan

Tom Fox and The National Catholic Reporter–Kansas

Nicki Pombier, Kate Kroeger, David Morrison, and the NetAid Foundation-New York

Rene Hansen and PACT–Zimbabwe

Dr. Gadner Michaud and Pathfinder International-Haiti

Aaron Hawks, Bob Eivan, Pablo Andrade, and Photographer Supply–San Francisco

Johnathan Falk and Project Empathy–www.projectempathy.org

Kimberly Lehn and Speer Girls High School–South Korea

Robin Bram, Marjory Werstuk, and STA Travel–San Francisco

Jane Wales and The World Affairs Council–San Francisco

Lucia Colmes, Andrea Henkart, Parviz Farouzgar, Sunderam Freeman, Jill Lublin, Garrett and Angie Mumma, Roderick Sun, and Barry Spilchuk.

To those of you that volunteered your time to collect or translate letters, my deepest gratitude: Walusimbi Willy–Uganda, Igor Letychevsky–Ukraine, Mrs. Oyenike Arike Adeyemo–Nigeria, Said Ndee–Tanzania, Mohamed Doofesh–Jordan, Walid Jamil–Lebanon, Victoria Egan–China, John Lava–Guinea Bissau, Rita Monteiro–India, Mangalagiri Nanda Ankur–India

Thank you for your help! Jamey Austin, Mike Baker, Joel Berman, Colin Carpenter, Katie Cooper, David Cornsweet, Matthew Cosgriff, Shannon Danilovich, Mike Davis, Johnathan Falk, Dan Fox, Terri Fox, Brian Geller, Tom Hamilton, Brooks Jordan, Emily Jordan, Marc Bamuthi Joseph, Leah Joy, Harris Masket, Sirena Masket, Janelle McCuen, Gabe Mott, Eric Rubin, Bruce Suggs, KLN Swami, Mary Swanson, Laura Tabet, Ora Weil, Dean Wolf, Suzanne Wolf, and Sabina Wyss.

To Dr. Michael Mamas, thank you for guiding my way.

To learn more about Letters to America. Please visit our Website at www.letterstoamerica.com.

If you have any questions regarding LTA or the authors please write to info@letterstoamerica.net.

Erica Geller can be contacted at Erica@letterstoamerica.net.

The statistics used in this book were found at www.cia.gov, www.worldfacts.us, MSN Encarta, and Human Development Reports http:\\hdr.undp.org.